THE IN-BETWEEN
GOD

THE IN-BETWEEN GOD

WALTER SCRAGG

REVIEW AND HERALD PUBLISHING ASSOCIATION
Washington, DC 20039-0555
Hagerstown, MD 21740

This book was
Edited by Gerald Wheeler
Designed by Richard Steadham
Cover photos by The Genesis Project
Type set:11/12 Zapf

Printed in U.S.A.

R & H Cataloging Service
Scragg, Walter R. L., 1925-
    The In-between God.

    1. Holy Spirit—Biblical teaching. 2. Bible.
N.T. Acts—Criticism, interpretation, etc.
I. Title.
BS2545.H62S37   1986   226'.606   86-28039

ISBN 0-8280-0374-2

"The Helper will come—the Spirit, who reveals the truth about God and comes from the Father. I will send him to you from the Father, and he will speak about me. And you, too, will speak about me, because you have been with me from the very beginning."

—John 15:26, 27, TEV

To Jan and Bert

Contents

Introduction

How could a cadre of committed persons, smaller even than Gideon's legendary 300, expect to conquer the world for their Lord? Luke gives the story of their valiant efforts and final victory in his second volume, The Acts of the Apostles. The Spirit flamed in their lives. The shout of conviction resounded. The trumpet of certainty shook multitudes in the camp of the enemy.

At the close of Luke's second volume the gospel has reached Rome, the center of the world. Jerusalem now fades away as a focus for the Christian gospel. The power of the Spirit floods out from new communities of faith scattered around the Mediterranean.

If the strongholds of Judaism lie open to the new torah of the Son of God, then the Spirit may claim that victory. And if the bastions of paganism and Roman cultism have become the camp of the new Israel of God, then the Power from on high must receive the honor.

In the book of Acts the Spirit mediates between the church and the world, within the church and within the world. Under His influence the world reversed itself and went down new pathways of faith. With solutions of startling newness in outreach and witness, the early band of Christian believers won enormous victories, because the Spirit went between them and the world.

Jesus had said, "Tarry ye in the city of Jerusalem, until ye be endued with power from on high" (Luke 24:49). He had spoken of the Spirit at work in the world: "And when he is come, he will reprove the world of sin, and of righteousness, and of judgment" (John 16:8). The band in the upper room found how true that was. Under His guidance issues that might have torn the little remnant apart proved to be doors to a new and greater outreach. The new theology of the kingdom took shape. Signposts from the Spirit pointed the leaders of that movement down the narrow path of truth and right living. The followers of Jesus moved ever further from the legalism of distorted Judaism and the frivolities of Greek and Roman paganism.

The Spirit is the "In-between God," the one who goes between, mediating, enabling, persuading. The discerning eye acknowledges that the world still survives only because of Him. Without Him the earth would have self-destructed long before this.

He has never stopped His work within the church. When apostate forces tore up the charter of truth during the pagan infiltrations of the Dark and Middle Ages, the winds of oppression and persecution scattered the pieces in a seemingly hopeless confusion. But the Spirit stayed with the church and, fragment by fragment, guided as faithful men and women searched out the lost scraps and re-created the original.

The church has not grown tired of its task. We know today that the ends of the earth wait outside our doors. The Spirit acts with us and for us as we go on divine errands of grace. In the gospel mission to a decadent and decaying world, He is God on our side.

But Luke would be appalled if we acclaimed the Spirit and failed to point to the One who has made the Spirit ours. Jesus had said, "I will pray the Father, and he shall give you another Comforter . . . even the Spirit of truth" (John 14:16, 17). "I send the promise of my Father upon you," He reassured (Luke 24:49). To the pre-Pentecost fledglings He urged, "Wait for the promise of the Father" (Acts 1:4).

The Acts of the Apostles are first the acts of Jesus, second the acts of the Spirit, and third the acts of the witnesses. From His position of power and privilege (Acts 7:55) Jesus has sent the Spirit to operate in and through the witnesses.

In Acts themes familiar from Luke continue, new notes sound, but the harmony the Spirit creates between God and man plays on. Under the Baton of Power the unknowing world responds precisely when God would have it orchestrated into His symphony. Within the church discord modulates to harmony. At His beck more and more instruments yield to His control.

The Godhead has given us Themselves in the Spirit. He goes in between us and all that God would accomplish. All is planned, all is known. Help, hope, joy, and love—the Spirit is what Jesus was to the world of Galilee and Judea. And He is ours.

Prelude
to Pentecost

Acts 1:1-4:12

A manuscript market of the first century, if available to Christians, would have contained both *Luke's Acts of Jesus* and *Luke's Acts of the Apostles.*

Luke wrote with decided goals in mind, wanting to continue the connected narrative he began in volume one. He wrote his Gospel to give authentic knowledge about Jesus (Luke 1:1-4). His second book, with its history of the church's birth, shows similar care.

The theological purposes of Acts develop out of the Gospel. If Luke shows Jesus as Saviour of the world, Acts explains how the world came to know Him as Saviour. Luke journeys Jesus from Galilee to heaven; Acts chronicles the results of that journey. The Gospel puts Jesus in conflict with established religion, while Acts establishes Christianity as the way to the kingdom. The first book identifies the men and women whom Jesus chose to be His witnesses, while the second volume proves the wisdom of His choices.

Promise and Power
Acts 1:1-26

At airports and truck terminals, at farming fairs and construction sites, the great monsters of the machine age wait quietly. Skill and technical wizardry have given them the potential of enormous power. They can fly 300 tons 5,000 miles; haul great loads across a continent; plow a county in a week; or claw their way into the stone heart of the earth.

But what if man himself is the tool, and God has His hand on the control?

"And, behold, I send the promise of my Father upon you: but tarry ye in the city of Jerusalem, until ye be endued with power from on high" (Luke 24:49).

Jerusalem had put the church's Lord on the cross. Its rulers had covered up the Resurrection. Threat hung over the disciples. If the Master had met death, what might the servants expect?

Judaism had proved its success as a world religion, capturing hundreds of thousands of proselytes and adherents in the most aggressive outreach it would ever know. Jerusalem thronged with the success of their mission. And its leaders knew how to pull up the drawbridge and defend the castle of faith. Pharisee might argue with Sadducee, Zealot compete with Essene, but in the crunch religious solidarity would exclude anything that seemed to threaten them.

Samaria ringed its faith with the fortifications of the Pentateuch. The Samaritans cloaked themselves in ultraconservatism. Not for them the proselytizing drive into the Roman Empire. While Israel sought new strength from expansion, Samaria tried to outdo the Jews in orthodoxy.

Rome and Greece readily melded new religions into old, blunting the edge of enthusiasm. Greece had its pantheon of gods, well able to fit in another one or two. Rome knelt before its god-emperor, the new Jove, who assumed priority over all other gods.

Into this world, this Jerusalem, this Judea and Samaria, this Rome and Greece, the Spirit would enter. The in-between One would amplify the feeble faith of the disciples, going before them and with them. The Divine Opportunist would seize every opening for Christ.

That world provided the very moment for the Spirit to make known His power:

1. Roman legions imposed unity on one of the largest concentrations of people in the history of the world.

2. Rome provided an unusually stable government and a long period of peace during which Christianity took root. Optimism about the future infected the people.

"The state did, in fact, claim the right . . . to decide which gods might be worshipped, but it did not trouble itself about a man's private opinions. . . . Christianity, which was first regarded as a movement within the permitted framework of Judaism, was at first unharmed by state action." [1]

3. Philosophy, religion, and the arts spoke and wrote Greek, a language marvelous in subtlety and rich in vocabulary.

The promise of expanding witness outlines the structure of Acts 1:8-11. Here the spiritual and symbolic combine with the factual and the literal. The kingdom of Christ makes Him King of kings, as well as placing the witness to His kingdom in all the world. God broke through into history when Gabriel announced the conception of Jesus. Again He did it through the Spirit as He came to the disciples (John 14:18, 19).

Mary (Acts 1:14) experienced again at Pentecost a personal acquaintance with the power and presence of the Holy Spirit. Her unique experiences lie beyond our comprehension. The presence of the women in the upper room continued Luke's interest in their role. Jesus' relatives would have included wives of His half brothers and perhaps their children.

Witness to the Resurrection (verse 22) dominated the disciples' motives. Luke centered his theology in the Resurrection. All the major speeches of Acts hinge around the event. The Son of man sits at the right hand of God because of it. As the risen Lord, Jesus activates the Spirit's power. Controversy between Christian witnesses and Jewish and Gentile antagonists explodes over the Resurrection. Belief in the risen Lord certifies the faith of a witness.

While the 120 prayed and fellowshipped in the upper room (verse 15), other disciples pondered and prayed elsewhere. We know Jesus appeared to 500 (1 Cor. 15:6). The three years of work in Galilee had produced a considerable following. Not for nothing were the early Christians called Galileans (Acts 1:11; 2:7; 13:31).

The Wind From God's Presence
Acts 2:1-13

Pentecost means "fiftieth," a reference to Leviticus 23:15, 16. The festival of the first fruits fell on the "[day] after the seventh Sabbath," or the fiftieth day after Passover. Jews of Jesus' day kept it as the anniversary of the giving of the Law at Mount Sinai.

At Pentecost devout Jews rejoiced in the giving of the Ten Commandments and the Law of Moses.[2] In a striking antitype the Spirit descended at Pentecost. Standing in a similar relationship to the Christian as the Law to the Jew, He guides, instructs, motivates, and directs. He does not abolish the ten, but applies them to the life as Jesus commanded in the Sermon on the Mount. While Moses received the Law from God, in Acts the witnesses received the Spirit (Acts 2:1, 2).

Jesus paralleled the Spirit with the wind (John 3:8). The Spirit is like a wind that separates the chaff from the grain (Luke 3:16, 17). This "rushing mighty wind" (Acts 2:2) filled the upper room. He is also a fire that consumes the chaff (Luke 3:17). The tongues of fire (Acts 2:3) affirmed that these faithful ones were God's true grain; the fire did not burn them up.

Did the disciples speak in the ecstatic utterances of 1 Corinthians 12-14? Or did they use foreign languages? Luke reported the latter, using a Greek verb connoting clarity of speech and understanding (Acts 2:4). He employs it again in Acts 2:14 to describe Peter's speech and in Acts 26:25, where it portrays Paul's speech.

People in the crowded streets heard the rushing wind and ran to the spot. It was not the roar of the wind, but the experience of hearing their own language spoken that bewildered them (Acts 2:6). Galileans had difficulty with guttural sounds and ran their words together (verse 7). The people of Jerusalem considered them provincial and unlearned (verses 7, 8). Thus it was a surprise to hear them speaking fluently in other languages.

At the very time when the church needed Him most to go in between the disciples and the skeptical crowds, God the Spirit mediated the gift of languages. For such timely gifts we entreat Him today.

But not even the miraculous convinces all (verses 12, 13). If the miracle would do its work, then the heart must receive it. The God-fearers and the Jews (verses 5, 12) from the Dispersion responded positively, wondering at the meaning of the miracle. The spiritually insensitive, among them some who put Jesus on the cross, mocked and said the preachers were drunk (verse 13).

Peter Says It for God
Acts 2:14-47

Peter presented the Christian gospel simply and directly: 1. The Spirit worked through the apostles in answer to Old Testament prophecy (Acts 2:16-21). 2. The descent of the Holy Spirit marked especially "the last days" (verse 17). 3. God singled out Jesus of Nazareth and put His stamp on Him through the signs and miracles He performed (verse 22). 4. After the execution of Jesus, God raised His Son to life again, thus defeating death (verse 24). 5. According to the plan of God, repentance would bring life to Israel (verses 23, 36). 6. Jesus now reigns at the right hand of God (verses 33-35). 7. All who hear ought to repent and be baptized for the forgiveness of sins (verse 38).

Peter drew from Joel and the Psalms in his address to the crowd, quoting many familiar passages (Ps. 16:8-11;

Joel 2:28-32). The Jews of his day saw at least two possibilities for a change in the fortunes of Israel. The Holy Spirit (Acts 2:33) might reawaken the prophetic gift and provide new Elijahs, Joels, and Isaiahs to point the people in the paths of righteousness. Or God might send the Messiah to give Israel its promised land of peace and plenty.

"The outpouring of the Spirit in the days of the apostles was the beginning of the early, or former, rain, and glorious was the result. To the end of time the presence of the Spirit is to abide with the true church. But near the close of earth's harvest, a special bestowal of spiritual grace is promised to prepare the church for the coming of the Son of man." [3]

This latter rain will fall from the bright clouds of God's promises (Zech. 10:1). It will supplement and complement the former rain (Joel 2:23).

Said Peter, "Save yourselves from this crooked generation" (Acts 2:40, RSV). Was it as bad as that? "Greece had already gone. The glory of Platonism had faded into the lesser glory of Neoplatonism. Jerusalem was as good as gone. The Jews had made a contribution of inestimable worth to the world, namely, the gift of ethical monotheism. . . . But they had rejected their greatest Son and missed their most pregnant opportunity. . . . [Rome] was becoming a vulture. It was losing its soul." [4]

The ship of the world drifts rudderless, Peter was saying. His generation has no lifeboat to save itself, or port to find shelter in. The storms mount higher and higher, the winds toss, and the waves swamp. The cry goes out, "Save yourselves," but the voice of faith responds, "Jesus saves."

Dear Name! Sweet Name!
Acts 3:1-26

"There's no other name like Jesus,
'Tis the dearest name we know,

'Tis the angel's joy in heaven,
'Tis the Christian's joy below." [5]

At the Gate Beautiful the name of Jesus showed its power (Acts 3:6). To act in the name of someone meant acknowledging your representative status. You were not the miracle worker, but the steward of the name that possessed that power. The witnesses carried the signet ring of the kingdom.

To the glory of the name of Jesus the Spirit lends His aid. He operates between the witness and the world to exalt Jesus and make His name effective.

"The work of the Spirit is not of a different order from that of Jesus. As the Lord taught His disciples the truth about Himself (John 14:6, 16-18), so will the Spirit of truth teach, guide, and correct (John 15:26; 16:13)." "It is a contradiction in terms and a confusion of experiences to consider oneself a Christian and yet have doubts as to whether the Spirit is present and operative in one's life. Paul said, 'If a man does not possess the Spirit of Christ he is no Christian (Rom. 8:9)." [6]

The Saviour, Jesus, gave healing power through the use of His name (Acts 3:6). That name stood over against the material value of silver and gold, which cannot heal or save. Nothing can match the name of Jesus—only in Him can any person find salvation (Acts 4:12). Jesus deplored the human tendency to rely on wealth.

"Leaping up" (Acts 3:8) is an ancient medical term for the socketing together of the ankle and heel. Only surgery (unavailable back then) and months of tedious healing could have accomplished what happened in a split second. The miracle would lose its value if the crowd imagined it originated with Peter and John (verse 12).

Peter created a sequence of venerable names intended to convey the nature and authority of Jesus' work: 1. The God of Abraham, Isaac, and Jacob had come in Jesus (verse 13). 2. Jesus is "his servant" (verse 26, RSV), an allusion to Isaiah 52:13. Therefore, Jesus is the sin-bearing servant of whom Isaiah spoke (Isa. 53). 3. Furthermore, Jesus is the Holy One (Acts 3:14), the God who redeems (Isa. 31:1; 41:14). Peter thus declared the deity and sinlessness of Jesus. 4. He is also the Righteous One (Acts 3:14, RSV), whose deeds match perfectly His nature.

Out of the events of Acts 2 and 3 grew the gift of boldness that carried the early believers through crisis after crisis. If the Spirit had not placed that gift between them and those who sought to deny their witness, the early church might have withered away. But emboldened by the gifts of Pentecost, reassured by the baptism of 3,000 people, exultant at the healing of the cripple, a feeling of supreme confidence filled them.

Boldness—The Spirit's Gift
Acts 4:1-12

Luke leads us to the climax of Acts 4:13, where being with Jesus produces boldness in the disciples. The argument of Acts runs like this: Jesus reigns with God and gives His Spirit to His church; to have the Spirit is to have Jesus; to have Jesus is to have power. Therefore, be bold. Therefore, witness. Therefore, put away fear and timidity.

The Resurrection created boldness. The new life they had from Jesus had delivered them from spiritual death. Pentecost people are resurrected people—crucified with Christ and risen with Him. Through their forceful witness all may experience resurrection to bold faith.

And if the power of the Holy Spirit (Acts 4:7) directed the witness to the power of the Resurrected, what earthly force could resist? The Resurrected and the Spirit filled the life so that the name of Jesus Christ not only heads the divine *Who's Who* but also heals, forgives, and transforms.

The Spirit has given us a new Peter, a new John, new apostles and disciples. Working within and between the members of that early company, He has created a cohesive, potent mixture made up of faith and confidence, witness and success, that sustained the beginners and still sustains us today.

If all this be true, who can deny our need to participate in witness? And who can contradict the supreme declaration of Acts 4:12: "And there is salvation in no one else; for there is no other name under heaven that has been given among men, by which we must be saved" (NASB)?

[1] E. M. Blaiklock, *Acts: An Introduction and Commentary*, p. 26.

[2] Frank E. Gaebelein, ed., *The Expositor's Bible Commentary*, vol. 9, p. 269.

[3] Ellen G. White, *The Acts of the Apostles*, pp. 54, 55.

[4] *The Interpreter's Bible*, vol. 9, pp. 44, 45.

[5] F. E. Belden, "There's No Other Name," *The Church Hymnal*, No. 517.

[6] Jan Paulsen, *When the Spirit Descends*, pp. 62, 64.

Witnesses All Are We

Acts 4:13-5:42

They stood and sang where the ferries disgorged the cross-harbor traffic. Ten of them in all, young except for one or two. My wife and I watched with the few and the curious fringing the group. I turned away an offer of a free *Steps to Christ* with a "We already have a copy at home."

Then one of them asked, "Would you come and join us?" How long was it since we had shared in street witnessing? I remembered Adelaide in 1947, and Betty thought of Melbourne about the same time. We sang along with them, handed out copies of *Steps to Christ*, and then left the intrepid band to continue their stand until the opera house crowds dispersed.

Because the Spirit holds us together in witness, we do not go on by as observers but share our faith. The commonality of witness both binds us together and moves us toward the world and its need.

What Can Stop Our Witness?
Acts 4:13-22

The Resurrection and Pentecost sent the disciples into mission and witness. Until the Resurrection they could neither understand nor accept the predictions about the suffering Messiah. And until Pentecost the horizon of discipleship stopped with the promise of the descent of the Spirit. Since then, their horizon had shifted to the completion of a world work.

How did the Spirit go between the witnesses and the

observers? What impact did He have?

1. The crowds "saw the boldness of Peter and John" (Acts 4:13).

2. The Resurrection and Pentecost took away doubt, cowardice, inhibitions, and low self-esteem.

3. The Spirit gave authority and conviction to "untrained laymen" (verse 13, NEB). "Their union with Him was stronger now than when He was with them in person. The light and love and power of an indwelling Christ shone out through them, so that men, beholding, marveled." [1]

4. The contrast between their boldness and their humble background provoked wonder—how did these men become what they now were (verse 13)?

5. The rulers came to a conclusion that filled them with alarm: these men had the essential character and powerful presence of Jesus (verse 13).

Not too long ago the same rulers had themselves faced Him, so wise and irresistible, though untrained (John 7:15). They had sensed an authority beyond their ken (Mark 1:22). The Spirit, sent by Jesus, gave similar wisdom and authority to the apostles. Not willing to concede what this meant about Jesus, the rulers kept quiet.

The Spirit offered a choice to the rulers, elders, and doctors of the law. He had convicted them of righteousness. Would they repent? The witnesses learned early that the gift of the Spirit did not give them coercive power over men. The Inquisition is no arm of the Spirit—each must make his own free decision.

The Sanhedrin, combining its religious and political authority, sought to restrain activities they thought damaging to the common good (Acts 4:17, 18). But Peter and John rejected the authority of the council. It was not God (verse 19), nor His representative. Pentecost had made God's will known—the disciples must speak and teach in the name of Jesus (verse 20; see Rom. 13:1-7).

Perceiving the Great Controversy
Acts 4:23-31

Having perceived that God was progressing His own plan, the church began a psalm of victory (Acts 4:24-30), like the songs and psalms in Luke 1 and 2.

The Greek word for sovereign is *despota* (verse 24). In Luke 2:29 Simeon declared, "Lord *[despota]*, now lettest thou thy servant depart in peace." In Acts the same sovereign Lord holds His servants (Acts 4:29) responsible for witness to the "holy child" (verse 27). Witness to Jesus is the solemn obligation of the Lord's servants.

Forces were aligning themselves against God and His purposes (verses 27, 28), but the sovereign Lord would give boldness to His servants as they witnessed (verse 29). In similar crises divine pulses will surge through the church showing how God is using and favoring His people today (Rev. 14:12).

The disciples saw in the servant songs of Isaiah 52 and 53 the true fate of Jesus (Acts 4:27). They, His servants, also suffered, but they would eventually reign with God along with their Master.

In answer to prayer the Spirit again filled the assembly (verse 31). As at Pentecost the messengers went into the streets in a wave of bold and fearless witness.

Response to the Resurrection
Acts 4:32-5:12

In Acts 3:5, 6 Peter and John rejected money as a source of power. The name of Jesus could save where silver and gold had no value. The early Christians' repudiation of a money-oriented movement produced a remarkable society of which Luke gives two examples. Barnabas disposed of his estate and brought the money to the apostles (verses 36, 37). Ananias and Sapphira also sold their property, but held back on giving all (Acts 5:1, 2).

Jesus had spoken of the power of love (Luke 6:27-32). He had shown love to all on the cross. Now that love saturated the lives of the early Christians. Not that they did not respect each other's property. Rather, they regarded each other's need as an opportunity to love by sharing with them.

Their lifestyle added to their witnessing effectiveness (Acts 4:34). The beggar by the gate called Beautiful no longer sat and begged. The name of Jesus both healed his crippled feet and gave him the ability to meet his everyday needs.

Already elements of church order were appearing. The common sharing permitted the apostles to give full time to witness (verse 32). They also had the responsibility for managing the church's funds (verse 35).

The elements of the great controversy, seen in the threat against Peter and John (verses 24-30), now receive further development. The book of Acts shows that human action has two possible prompters. Barnabas (verses 36, 37) had the Spirit to thank for his commitment to the common cause. Ananias and Sapphira yielded their lives to Satan's control (Acts 5:3). While Barnabas, the Spirit's man, went on to witness and triumph for Christ, Ananias and his wife suffered judgment (verses 5, 10), a fate reserved for all who persist in refusing the Spirit.

In Jerusalem the people knew only too well how the rulers ran things. Jesus Himself had pointed up their selfishness and greed (Luke 20:45-47). But in the kingdom of the Spirit love and generosity reigned. And the people knew it. In that kingdom power emerged to heal and redeem (Acts 5:11, 12).

Luke appreciates the wider implications of the Spirit's activity. Ananias lies to the Spirit (verse 3); the Spirit upholds the church (Acts 9:31); the Spirit sets Barnabas and Saul apart for the work to which He has called them; the Spirit makes a decision about demands on Gentile believers (Acts 15:28). Thus Luke shows us the Spirit as divine person, even though he does not emphasize the personal activity of the Spirit in the life of the individual believer.

> "Holy Spirit, faithful Guide,
> Ever near the Christian's side,
> Gently lead us by the hand,
> Pilgrims in a desert land;
> Weary souls fore'er rejoice,
> While they hear that sweetest voice,
> Whispering softly, 'Wanderer, come!
> Follow Me, I'll guide thee home.' " [2]

The Good News Advances
Acts 5:17-42

The church would know many occasions when jealous power structures sought by punitive action to contain further expansion. Solomon's Portico, a covered colonnade on the eastern side of the outer court of the Temple, had become the place for planning and counsel (Acts 5:12). From it Peter moved out into the streets, witnessing and healing (verse 15). The fame of the new movement spread out into Judea, and the people surged into Jerusalem with their sick and found healing (verse 16).

The attractiveness of the alternative offered by the band of apostles and their followers threatened the authority of the Sanhedrin, led by Sadducean priests. They swooped on the headquarters of the Christian community and swept all 12 of the apostles into prison (verses 17, 18). But the question still nagged away at the Sanhedrin, Are these troublemakers or do they represent God's will (verses 38, 39)?

"The disciples were but humble men, without wealth, and with no weapon but the Word of God; yet in Christ's strength they went forth to tell the wonderful story of the manger and the cross, and to triumph over all opposition.

Without earthly honor or recognition, they were heroes of faith. From their lips came words of divine eloquence that shook the world." [3] And so it may be today.

"Luke now speaks resumptively of three groups of people and their response to the Sanhedrin's warning and the fear engendered by Ananias and Sapphira's fate: (1) the Christians and their continued meeting together in Solomon's Colonnade; (2) the unbelieving Jews *(hoi polloi,* "the rest") and their reluctance to associate too closely with the Christians; and (3) the responsive Jews *(ho laos,* "the people") and their honoring the Christians—with, in fact, many men and women from this group coming to believe in the Lord and being added to the number of Christian believers." [4]

The tragedy of Ananias and Sapphira must have had an inhibiting effect on the believers. In part their courage had recovered as the apostles' work brought new success (verse 16). Now the Sadducees acted against the twelve (verses 17, 18). Was it another evidence of divine displeasure? What a tonic when the angel led the apostles out of the prison (verse 19)! Even better, he commanded them to return to Solomon's Portico and get on with their preaching (verse 20). A sense of the miraculous and the divine presence has always accompanied the successful spread of the gospel.

Can you imagine the chagrin of the Sanhedrin as the report came from the jailers (verses 22, 23)? And the fear that report brought? The apostles and their followers were growing in strength and popularity.

Distances were not great in ancient Jerusalem, and the apostles soon stood before the Sanhedrin (verses 26, 27). Peter had earlier said in his sermon, "Whom ye crucified" (Acts 4:10), forcing the leaders to recognize the role they had played in Jesus' death. Not only did the accusation lay blame on the Sanhedrin, but it appeared to the council that the apostles were seeking divine retribution on them for their deed (Acts 5:28).

The shadow of Stephen's martyrdom falls back across these pages. The apostles, like Stephen, would die at the hands of their enemies. They might escape for now, but the threat had clearly emerged—the rulers had already acted, and would strike against them again.

Peter replied with a declaration of belief (verses 29-32). It included (1) the Crucifixion (verse 30); (2) the Resurrection (verse 30); (3) the Ascension (verse 31); (4) the reign at the right hand of God (verse 31); (5) Jesus' role as leader and Saviour (verse 31); (6) the doctrines of repentance and forgiveness (verse 31); (7) the witnessing church (verse 32); and (8) the gift of the Holy Spirit (verse 32).

The apostles benefited from the intervention of the highly esteemed Gamaliel (verse 34). But even without him they may have had supporters. Paul later said that many of the Jerusalem believers were "zealous for the law" (Acts 21:20). The believers had shown themselves faithful to the Temple (Acts 3:1). It was Stephen's view of the law and the Temple that brought him to trial (Acts 6:14). But in this hearing (Acts 5:34) Peter and the apostles did not face such accusations.

"The Jerusalem Christians were faithful to the Temple and to 'the customs that Moses delivered to us.' It was presumably this loyalty to and observance of the Torah, both written and oral, that transformed the Pharisees' opposition to Jesus into much more tolerant acquiescence toward the activities of His followers (Acts 5:33-39) and that attracted many Pharisees into the new sect while still remaining Pharisees (Acts 15:5; 21:20)." [5]

Gamaliel's mention of Theudas (Acts 5:36) poses a problem. The only known Theudas raised a rebellion in A.D. 44-46, after the time of this hearing. Josephus mentions him. Was Luke confusing the matter, or did Gamaliel have someone else in mind? Luke's reputation for accuracy far exceeds Josephus's, whom we know made errors and exaggerations. Judas (verse 37) rebelled in A.D. 6. His revolt did not succeed, but led to the founding of the Zealot movement.

Gamaliel, a highly revered Jewish rabbi, had a more humane and sympathetic interpretation of the Law than many other rabbis. His influence was great, and he swayed even the Sadducees to let the apostles go free. His apparent sympathy for their cause may be seen in his logical entreaty on their behalf in verses 38 and 39. Many Bible scholars believe Gamaliel favored the second alternative: that the apostles' work is of God, not from man.

Flogging rather than death brought relief and joy (verses 40, 41). They had no thought of obeying the injunction to stop preaching (verse 40), having already declared whom they would obey (verse 29). Only thus could they ensure the continued presence of the Spirit, who manifests Himself in power only through those who obey (verse 32).

And so the good news flourished. The apostles neither gave up their podium in the Temple nor softened their message. The joy that the good news of Jesus the Messiah was bringing continued and grew.

"What was the strength of those who in the past have suffered persecution for Christ's sake? It was union with God, union with the Holy Spirit, union with Christ. Reproach and persecution have separated many from earthly friends, but never from the love of Christ." [6]

---

[1] White, *The Acts of the Apostles*, p. 65.

[2] M. M. Wells, "Holy Spirit, Faithful Guide," *The Church Hymnal*, No. 211.

[3] White, *The Acts of the Apostles*, p. 77.

[4] James D. Dunn, *Unity and Diversity in the New Testament*, p. 64.

[5] Gaebelein, ed., *The Expositor's Bible Commentary*, vol. 9, p. 317.

[6] White, *The Acts of the Apostles*, p. 85.

Moving Out With the Spirit

Acts 6:1-8:3

The classic command at the moment of advance echoes throughout Acts, "Move out!"

The book recounts the derring-do of commanders who move ahead of their troops, of scouts promoted to generals, of supply staff who fight at the front line. Peter the bombast is transformed into Peter the bold. Paul the persecutor emerges as Paul the proclaimer.

Through the Spirit we may yet become far different from what we are now. That is the message for you and me. He permeates our weakness to make us strong. He bridges between us and opportunity so that Christ may have the glory.

The new movement would change the world. But up to this point it had remained stuck in Jerusalem. How would the Spirit move them out to "the uttermost part of the earth" (Acts 1:8)? Who would be the hero that leads the advance?

Speech as Witness

In Acts speeches play a similar role to the stories that fill the Gospel of Luke. None of them is as simple as it first seems. Each has an important purpose.

Even little speeches teach great truths. Peter declared loyalty to God as the supreme human obligation (Acts 4:19, 20). He asserted the sole and unique claims of Jesus on all men (verses 8-12), thus opening the thought world of the church to its universal mission. The unison speech or song of the believers explained events in an eternal framework (verses 24-30). And Peter declared the purpose God had for Israel in sending Jesus Christ (Acts 5:28-32).

All such speeches represent summaries. Luke does not always use the precise words that the originators used, but he never neglects the essence of the matter.

Generally, the major speeches in the book of Acts show the following similarity of structure:

1. They begin with direct address to the audience: "Ye men of Judaea" (Acts 2:14) or "Men and brethren" (verse 37). 2. The speaker appeals for earnest attention: "Be it known" (Acts 4:10) or "Hearken" (Acts 7:2; 15:13). 3. A misunderstanding must be put right (Acts 4:9; 3:12). 4. Quotes and examples from Scripture are frequent (Acts 7). 5. The message about Jesus Christ often appears in similar words or thoughts. 6. It focuses on the specific audience and their situation.[1]

The reasonable assumption is that Luke imposed structure on the sermon material that he had at hand. "Inspiration acts not on the man's words or his expressions but on the man himself, who, under the influence of the Holy Ghost, is imbued with thoughts. But the words receive the impress of the individual mind. The divine mind is diffused. The divine mind and will is combined with the human mind and will; thus the utterances of the man are the word of God."[2]

A Man Full of Faith
Acts 6:1-8

Peter and John repeatedly found themselves in trouble. And Stephen was the first to lose his life. Like these first Christians, countless thousands have trod, and are still treading, paths that lead to persecution and death for the sake of the Lord.

The story of Stephen begins with a practical issue. Common ownership depended on complete fairness and impartiality. The widows of the Greek-speaking Jews thought themselves badly treated as the leaders distributed supplies (Acts 6:1).

In the pressure of keeping the community stable the apostles had been forced away from their consuming passion for evangelism (Acts 4:33) to attend to internal problems (Acts 6:2). Supervising the distribution of food to a largely poor membership restricted their witness.

The twelve exercised authority in the community, speaking as one (verse 2). Unity in leadership prevailed, an important element in the success of the Christian movement.

If the twelve had appointed Stephen only to "serve tables," the Spirit had other ideas. The seven became for the Greek-speaking Jews what the twelve were for the Hebrew Christians. They soon gave up their role as administrators and, especially Stephen and Philip, became missionary preachers (verse 7).

Luke has no special interest in describing how the early church organized itself. "What Luke feels to be essential, therefore, is not to point out the origin of a constitutive office of the church, but to write an account of the church that is prepared to be shown new and unaccustomed ways and also to take them; and then individual members must be separated for these special tasks." [3]

The "deacons" (Acts 6 does not call them that) now provided a fresh impetus to the work of the church. Success mounted on success as "the word of God increased; and the number of the disciples multiplied . . . greatly; and a great company of the priests believed" (verse 7).

Understanding the God of Glory
Acts 6:8-7:43

Who had the right understanding of God? The Jews declared Stephen guilty of blasphemy against Moses and God (verse 11), and against the Temple and the Law (verse

13). Blasphemy defames the divine character and purposes. But Luke denies the charges against Stephen. Those who disputed with him bribed men to testify against him (verse 11). False witnesses (verse 13), they twisted what Stephen had said even as others had done at Jesus' trial (Mark 14:58).

Some in the Sanhedrin may have thought the apostles naive and deluded, their appeal to the masses soon to pass. But when Stephen attacked the very foundations of contemporary Judaism, there was no hope of holding back the angry council.

Luke describes Stephen as a new Moses whom the Sanhedrin in their blindness could not recognize. Just as Moses' face shone from his closeness to God, so Stephen's face assumed an unearthly character, glowing like an angel's (Acts 6:15).

Then Luke takes us from a man with glory on his face to the God of glory (Acts 7:2). Thus Stephen forced the Sanhedrin to recognize that the Christian message had the same source and authority as that of Moses. It came from the God of glory.

Stephen set up one of the pillars on which he would build his reasoning: the glory of God represented the special approval of God and was not confined to Palestine. It might appear anywhere—even in Mesopotamia (verse 2).

The second statement put up another pillar. God traveled with Abraham as he wandered; He dwelt with His chosen people wherever they pitched their tents (verse 3).

A third point emerges in verse 5. Abraham's true inheritance was in the promises God gave rather than in the land of Israel.

Stephen then proceeded to reinterpret Israel's history according to his three principles. The covenant of circumcision (verse 8) did not guarantee Abraham's descendants the land. His seed had to leave it (verse 9), but God traveled with them (verse 9). In fact, God could and did give great and special favor outside the borders of Israel. Joseph became governor of Egypt (verse 10).

The blessings of God so abounded in Egypt that the total number of the people of God—Jacob and his family—joined Joseph in Egypt, forsaking Canaan (verse 15). Joseph and Jacob were learning that their true inheritance lay in God and His blessing, not in geography.

The pilgrimage of Israel met a crisis as they multiplied in Egypt (verse 17). At the same time another factor emerged that also formed part of Stephen's reasoning. The promise of deliverance had a time limit on it (verse 17). In other words, God had a plan to which earthly events had to conform.

God urged upon Moses the plight of Israel (verse 23). Moses went on a mission of deliverance (verse 25), but his people actively rejected him (verse 27). By the end of his sermon Stephen will have made this a telling point: it was of the very nature of Israel to reject God's deliverers.

But the servant of God can go from one Gentile country to another and still have the God of glory with him. God blessed Moses with sons (verse 29) while in exile. He showed His glory in the burning bush (verse 30). Most important of all, He declared His holy name there in the wilderness, in isolation from the chosen people, and in a foreign land (verse 32).

In the turnaround that made God's second attempt at making Moses Israel's deliverer successful (verse 36; cf. verse 25), Stephen's listeners might have heard the silent appeal; you have rejected Jesus once, don't reject those who do His work today. He is coming to you even as I speak. Hear Him and accept His deliverance.

Even more, said Stephen, you know of the signs and wonders Moses performed and regard them highly (verse 36). Why then do you reject the signs and wonders done in the name of Jesus?

Stephen was not the first to idealize the wilderness experience of Israel (verse 38). However, he made sure that the audience would see how in the light of the dawning Christian era they should now interpret that marvelous time. Moses knew of the coming Prophet (verse 37) who would carry the nature of God. Israel should have recognized Jesus as the son in His parable of the vineyard (Luke 20:13, 14). Did the hearers begin to discern Stephen's direction at this point? Would they even now at this late date hear Him (Acts 8:37)?

> "Gracious God, my heart renew,
> Make my spirit right and true;
> Cast me not away from Thee,
> Let Thy Spirit dwell in me;
> Thy salvation's joy impart,
> Steadfast make my willing heart." [4]

The moment of rejection in Egypt had set a pattern. They spurned Moses the deliverer (Acts 7:39) and yearned for Egypt. Wanting nothing of God's latest plan, Israel sought to thwart it (verse 40). The people became idolaters rather than obey God's will (verses 40-42). The insignificant glory of the stars supplanted the God of glory, and the gruesome tabernacle of Moloch led them far from the tent of testimony (verses 43, 44).

When God Gives Up on Israel
Acts 7:44-8:2

What had sent them far off? A longing for a god they could use to their own ends. They would not submit to God's purposes for them any more than Stephen's audience would.

The tabernacle of witness proclaimed the name and character of God. The witness, or testimony, was the Ten Commandments (Ex. 31:18). The wilderness tabernacle came to them at God's initiative (Acts 7:44). Even the tabernacle David wished to construct had God's favor (verse 46). "But Solomon built him an house" (verse 47). And there the specter of apostasy reared over Israel.

In Stephen's analysis of Israel's failure the erecting of a material structure for God turned the people from the God of glory to the glory of a house. The Temple attracted the pride of Israel. They replaced idol worship with temple worship (verse 48). Seeking to tie God down to their will, they forgot His freedom (verse 49) and their own created status (verse 50). The Holy Spirit cannot penetrate a barrier of self-sufficiency (verse 51). How could God tolerate such arrogance?

Abraham, Joseph, Moses—Israel had patterned itself after none of them, but rather after the idolatrous nations around them. Moreover, they had killed the prophets (verse 52). And more recently they had done something even worse: having known the Law and the prophets and all that was written of the coming Messiah, they had not only rejected Him but had actually murdered "the Just One" (verse 52).

Neither Pharisee nor Sadducee escaped Stephen's scathing blast. It touched them and convicted them, but conviction brought fury, not remorse (verse 54).

But where was the God of glory now? And who must they hear if they would know His will? Stephen pointed heavenward and declared that he saw the Son of man standing on the right hand of God (verses 55, 56). For the Jewish leaders that meant judgment in session and against them (Dan. 7:13), while for Stephen it meant intercession in his favor and assurance of eternal life (Acts 7:59).

They rushed toward him (verse 57), shouting as they ran. Hounded out of the Temple precincts into the lanes behind the Temple, he had little hope of rescue (cf. Acts 21:31, 32). The mob trapped him outside the city walls. According to legal requirements for stoning, the first witness would push him off the cliff outside the wall into the valley below. The second witness would drop a boulder on him. Then others would rain stones on him until he died.

But they lynched Stephen. Stripping off their clothes (verse 58), they crippled him with stones and then pelted him to death. In the spirit of the prophets, like the true Prophet, he sought to turn aside the judgment of God, calling on the Lord to remove the guilt from his tormentors (verse 60).

Not only did A.D. 34 see the death of Christianity's first martyr, but it also sent the church into the four corners of the world. First Peter and then Paul would find their mission in a wider world.

Stephen's vision taught the church to look ever to heaven for intercession. Acts 7:56 links with Acts 1:10, 11. The company of believers knew that Jesus had ascended. They knew by faith and study that He reigned at the Father's right hand. The dying martyr confirmed their bright hopes, as he saw Jesus with God.

As for Saul, one of the initiators of Stephen's trial, he watched it all with satisfaction. And set about his nefarious work with even greater vigor. But the Lord at the right hand of God had seen and noted him. And God was not finished with him yet (Acts 8:1).

"For a time he was a mighty instrument in the hands of Satan to carry out his rebellion against the Son of God. But soon this relentless persecutor was to be employed in building up the church that he was now tearing down. A Mightier than Satan had chosen Saul to take the place of the martyred Stephen, to preach and suffer for His name, and to spread far and wide the tidings of salvation through His blood." [5]

---

[1] Eduard Schweizer, in L. E. Keck and J. L. Martyn, eds., *Studies in Luke-Acts*, pp. 210, 211.

[2] White, *Selected Messages*, book 1, p. 21.

[3] Eduard Schweizer, *Church Order in the New Testament*, p. 73.

[4] "God Be Merciful to Me," *The SDA Hymnal*, No. 297.

[5] White, *The Acts of the Apostles*, p. 102.

The Spirit as People Mover

Acts 8:3-9:31

Any personnel manager of a large organization can tell you the problems he faces in having people change jobs. Even a shift to the office next door can bring tears or anger.

The New Testament, and especially Acts, makes the Holy Spirit a people mover, not just in the sense that He motivates, but in the very practical sense of transferring people from one locality to another or from one task to another. Through such actions the Spirit showed that He could use those who trusted His control to advance the church's mission. Are you, the Bible asks, ready to accept the moving of the Spirit?

The Power of God Against the Power of Evil
Acts 8:3-25

The vision of Stephen taught that the Son of man had already received kingship from God (Dan. 7:13; Acts 7:56). God had declared Himself on the side of those who trusted in Jesus, both then and eternally. Whatever now happened could not alter that heavenly decision. Storms of hate and persecution might decimate the church on earth, but the victorious Jesus assured the witnesses of God's favor.

The Jews thoroughly despised the Samaritans and considered them as foreigners, like the Gentiles. They *did*, however, keep the Sabbath, honored the Pentateuch, and practiced circumcision.

The unnamed city in Samaria was probably the capital, Sebaste. To a man they listened eagerly to the deacon Philip (verses 5, 6). Like Nineveh in Jonah's time they responded, while many in Jerusalem quibbled and persecuted (verse 8; cf. Jonah 3:9, 10).

Philip's ministry brought healing to the demon possessed and physically ill (Acts 8:7, 8). In the same area Simon practiced his magical arts (verse 9).

"Simon the sorcerer, or Simon Magus as he is called in postapostolic Christian writings, was a leading heretic in the early church. Justin Martyr (died c. A.D. 165), who was himself a Samaritan, says that nearly all his countrymen revered Simon as the highest god. Irenaeus (c. A.D. 180) speaks of him as the father of Gnosticism and identifies the sect of the Simonians as being derived from him." [1]

How do we distinguish between the power of the Spirit and that of the occult?

The occult and the magical attempt to manipulate the natural course of events for their own benefit (verses 11, 18). In miracles God uses His own laws in extraordinary ways to fulfill His purposes (verses 12, 13). Magic seeks to subject one human will to another for the stronger's purposes (verse 19). A miracle seeks the will of God for another through submission to God's purposes (verse 16).

Simon had thrown up his hands and declared it no contest. He joined the other Samaritans and was baptized (verses 12, 13). But his baptism had the wrong motive: "He was carried away when he saw the powerful signs and miracles that were taking place" (verse 13, NEB). People can make good decisions for wrong reasons.

In a complex situation such as was developing, Philip needed help and counsel. He was "full of the Holy Ghost and wisdom" (Acts 6:3), but probably had not met an issue as complex as this. Peter and John, who had seen Jesus at work, soon arrived to confirm the converts (Acts 8:15).

At all costs Simon wanted the power that Peter and John had (verse 18). However we may seek to "buy" the

Spirit, we can never have Him at our choosing. Instead, He moves freely and gives at His own discretion. To seek Him for our own purposes or satisfaction, however worthy the motive, puts us under the condemnation that Simon received (verses 20, 21).

How did those Samaritans know they had received the Holy Spirit? Luke does not mention speaking in tongues, but simply the laying on of hands (verse 18).

While we cannot know whether the modern ecstatic utterance is the same as that described in 1 Corinthians 14, we do know that it differed sharply from that presented in Acts. One commentator describes the gift of the Spirit at Ephesus (Acts 19) this way: "They were then baptized in the name of Jesus, and as Paul 'laid his hands upon them,' they received also the baptism of the Holy Spirit, by which they were enabled to speak the languages of other nations and to prophesy. Thus they were qualified to labor as missionaries in Ephesus and its vicinity, and also to go forth to proclaim the gospel in Asia Minor." [2]

In his review of "tongues" (1 Cor. 14) Paul makes many negative comments:

1. No man understands what is said (verse 2). 2. Only the person himself is edified (verse 4). 3. It is better and greater to prophesy (verse 5). 4. Even a Paul speaking in tongues would not profit the church (verse 6). 5. Tongues give the trumpet an uncertain sound (verse 8). 6. Tongues speak to the air (verse 9). 7. Tongues provide no understanding (verse 14). 8. Five words with understanding are better than 10,000 in tongues (verse 19). 9. Tongues appear as insanity to outsiders (verse 23). 10. Without interpretation tongues have no purpose except for the individual (verse 28). 11. Tongues produce confusion (verse 33).

Luke gives great significance to the gift of foreign languages because it aided the witness and mission of the church that so interested him. Paul met a different situation in Corinth. Certainly we should not urge others or ourselves into the Corinthian situation.

A Model for Witnessing
Acts 8:26-40

Many times as I travel I see people reading religious literature. Given such an opportunity, Philip used it for God. He asked an innocent question, but one that left the way open for discussion: "Do you understand what you are reading?" (verse 30). The question offered no threat and is a model to all who wish to witness for Christ.

The story builds on the concern that Philip showed in what captivated the eunuch (verse 32, 33). Be interested in others if you would win them, Luke implies. Understand the Bible; be able to explain it. When someone wants to know, give a correct answer, and always point that person to Jesus Christ (verses 34, 35).

Jesus used Isaiah 53 to speak of His sufferings (Mark 10:45), identifying the suffering Servant with the Messiah who comes in David's line (Isa. 11), and with the Son of man (Dan. 7:13). He said, "How is it written of the Son of man, that he must suffer many things, and be set at nought" (Mark 9:12).

The earliest manuscripts of Acts finish simply with the baptism of the eunuch (Acts 8:36). Fuller, and perhaps later versions, throw an interesting light on early church practice. At the time of baptism the convert would be asked, "Do you believe in Jesus Christ with all your heart?" He would reply, "I believe that Jesus Christ is the Son of God" (see verse 37).

Philip, moved literally by the Spirit (verse 39), headed for another mission (verse 40). The eunuch went on his way filled also with the Spirit to witness among his people. As Philip journeyed north from Gaza, he preached as he went. Finally he settled in Caesarea, where Paul found him, with his family, some 20 years later (Acts 21:8). And what a family! His four daughters had the very gift that Paul cherished for the church—prophecy!

Jesus Calls a New Disciple
Acts 9:1-9

When Jesus said we are to forgive as He forgives, even to seventy times seven, He was giving an important principle of human relationships. We may have to keep forgiving the same person for the same wrong. Although we may not be able to forget, we can forgive.

Acts and the Epistles show that Paul could not forget his wrongs against Jesus. Sensing the newness and weakness of the fledgling Christian community, he had sought to squash it once and for all. The gracious forgiveness of Jesus gave Paul an overwhelming desire to make up for his attacks on the church.

One of the amazing features of the story is Ananias's willingness to forgive Paul and help him find acceptance in the church. God may turn a hard heart into the new creation of God.

The "way" as a term for Christianity occurs only in the book of Acts (Acts 9:2; 19:9, 23; 22:4; 24:14, 22). Luke speaks of the "way of the Lord" (Luke 3:4). The Pharisees asked Jesus about the "way of God" (Mark 12:14). Jesus called Himself "the way" (John 14:6).

Though those with him observed only a brilliant but diffused light (Acts 9:3), Paul, like Stephen, actually saw Jesus (Gal. 1:16; 1 Cor. 9:1) in a revelation from heaven (Acts 9:4; cf. 7:56).

Paul had found it hard to "kick against the pricks" (Acts 26:14). Stephen's vision of the Son of man, and his willingness to die for Jesus had impressed Paul. He had found relentless faith and sense of mission among those he persecuted (Acts 8:4).

The heavenly figure demanded, "Why are you persecuting me?" (See Acts 9:4.) Paul knew the figure to be the Lord (verse 5). As a devout Jew he accommodated fairly well to the sudden vision and the voice of divine authority. What left him in shock was the identity of the Person in the vision. In persecuting the Christians he was attacking Jesus (verse 5), the one who now reigned with God in heaven!

Life with God begins with such encounters. Jesus speaks through the Word and the Spirit; we tremble and weep, but He has a plan for us. Often He will send an Ananias to help us know what we should do.

The Spirit Has a Plan for All
Acts 9:10-31

What if the Spirit impresses you to go to your worst enemy? Ananias faced that choice when the Lord told him about Paul's conversion (Acts 9:11, 12). His reply, though, has a familiar ring. He used the same words as Samuel (verse 10; cf. 1 Sam. 3:4-9). In the same spirit Mary responded to Gabriel (Luke 1:38). The devout, obedient heart consents thus to the will of the Lord.

In Ananias's hesitation (Acts 9:13, 14) we have the natural reaction to a menace from outside the community. What fear Paul must have wrought! The simple words "and Ananias went" showed his open faith and complete trust (verse 17). Through such a man God might initiate mighty events (verses 15, 16).

God's plan for Ananias took him to a needy brother. Going in compassion (verse 17), he healed Saul (verse 18). Through him Paul received both sight and the Holy Spirit (verse 17). Ananias baptized Paul and helped him recover his strength (verse 19).

God chose Paul as His instrument of salvation for the Gentiles, their rulers, and for Israel itself (verse 15). In Galatians 1 Paul denied that he received his calling from any man—it came directly from God. This does not contradict God's use of Ananias. The disciple had no authority from Jerusalem or the apostles. Instead, he carried out exact instructions from Jesus.

The laying on of hands represented at least two

things. First, it showed Ananias's acceptance of Paul into the band of witnesses to Jesus. Second, it acknowledged the confession of faith Paul made. We should not see the laying on of hands as transmitting the Spirit to Paul. By giving Paul the Spirit, God showed that Ananias and the church had perceived his commitment correctly. Trust in Jesus and the gift of the Spirit accompany each other in the New Testament.

Paul immediately declared Jesus the Son of God (verse 20). His brilliant and forceful approach soon demonstrated its merits (verse 22). Yet for now he worked solely among the Jews, using cogent proofs to show that Jesus was the Messiah (verse 22).

Fiercely opposed in Damascus, Paul went into Arabia, probably shortly after Stephen's death, perhaps in late A.D. 34 or early A.D. 35. "Impatient men forget that God is not bound by time. His conversion was by far the most vital influence in Paul's life. Ancestry, Pharisaic training, Hellenistic education, were fused by it into the character that the Holy Spirit formed and fashioned over 14 years of training. At length, in God's good time, the door opened, and the events of half a lifetime assumed final and complete significance." [3]

Again and again in his Epistles Paul assured his readers that God has a plan that He is working out. He could never doubt it. From the experience of his own life he could offer assurance to others. And so may all who trust and obey!

Damascus, though a haven for a time, finally proved too dangerous. Paul escaped by night and fled to Jerusalem (verses 23, 24).

Two kindhearted men played key roles in assuring Paul's future. First Ananias, and later Barnabas, surrounded him with affectionate support. Barnabas had that magnanimous spirit that will take a person as they appear and profess to be (verses 26, 27). He believed Paul's story about the vision on the way to Damascus and accepted the reports of the new apostle's preaching in that city. On the word of this good and godly man the Jerusalem church welcomed Paul.

But Jerusalem had no part in God's plan for Paul at this time (Acts 22:18-21). God did not want him as a second Stephen (Acts 9:29), though Paul was willing to face that danger.

Comparison of the events in Acts with Paul's own record in Galatians leaves unanswered questions that have puzzled Bible scholars for centuries. Two comments may help. First, a historian like Luke may give greater importance to an event than the individual himself. Second, a man like Paul, with an intense sense of how God had led him according to a specific plan, may have excluded from his autobiography details that seemed unimportant to that plan.

Looking at the way God used events to shape the life of Paul makes us aware how much we need to trust God through His Spirit. The Spirit bestowed on Ananias the gift of courage to meet the archenemy of the faith. He gave the gift of encouragement and compassion to Barnabas so that despite the doubts of others, Paul's ministry might continue. For Philip, for Paul, for the church, the Spirit was moving people. Will He move me? Will He move you?

---

[1] Gaebelein, ed., *The Expositor's Bible Commentary*, vol. 9, p. 358.

[2] White, *The Acts of the Apostles*, p. 283.

[3] Blaiklock, *Acts: An Introduction and Commentary*, p. 90.

No More People-filing

Acts 9:32-11:30

Are you a person-filer? Do you have a way of attaching a label to a person and filing him away with other people that have the same classification? Simple things may create categories of people: the color of their eyes and skin, the clothes they wear, the way they style their hair, how much of their facial hair they shave off.

That's quite a normal way to deal with a complex and varied world. But we can take it a dangerous step further by attaching moral or social values to simple things that would normally just describe a person's appearance. We do it with race, with religion, with occupations, with educational levels—just about anything that might describe a person can receive a negative or positive value.

Jesus spoke out against people-filing. He would have nothing to do with grading the eternal value of Pharisee or Sadducee, shepherd or scribe, tanner or tax collector. All needed the saving grace of God in equal measure.

Jesus Christ Cures You
Acts 9:32-43

With Paul, now a champion of the Christian cause, at home in Tarsus (Acts 9:30), peace came to the young church (verse 31). Witness flourished. The Jerusalem church in dispersion evangelized all the surrounding areas. Two factors contributed to successful evangelism. First, all activities related to God and His will were undertaken "in the fear of the Lord" (verse 31). And second, the church was "upheld by the Spirit," who provided motivation and support (verse 31, NEB).

Luke now offers two examples of what the Lord was bringing about in the church through the Spirit. 1. Jesus Christ cured Aeneas (verse 34). To cure meant to remove sin as well as make well. Many would have thought Aeneas a great sinner because his illness was chronic (verse 33).

2. The story of Dorcas (verses 36-38) illustrates how important women were in the service and ministry of the early church. Later we will meet Priscilla, the senior partner in an evangelistic duo, and the four daughters of Philip, prophetesses to the church.

Luke's evaluation of Dorcas's ministry has encouraged the creation of more than one movement to aid the poor and disadvantaged. Typical responses include Adventist Community Services and the Adventist Development and Relief Agency (ADRA).

Both Elijah and Elisha brought life to the dead, the miracle taking place in the prophet's roof chamber, or upper room (1 Kings 17:19; 2 Kings 4:10, 21). In Peter's miracle (verse 39) the body also lay in an upper room. Those who put it there would have remembered other upper room experiences.

The region around Joppa had a semi-Gentile population. The response to these miracles took the gospel a further half step toward the Gentile world (Acts 9:42).

We should not think that all that was needed for conversion was a miracle. The Lord had commanded the disciples to "teach all nations" (Matt. 28:19). Behind the large numbers that came to the faith lay a program of indoctrination, and following that, baptism.

Peter lodged with a tanner, one of the professions thought by the Pharisees to be incapable of freedom from ritual pollution (Acts 9:43). Aeneas, sick beyond a cure, Dorcas, a dead woman, and now Simon, a tanner, showed how Christianity rejects traditional people-filing.

"In Christ now meet both east and west,
In Him meet south and north;
All Christly souls are one in Him
Throughout the whole wide earth." [1]

Accepting the Unacceptable
Acts 10:1-43

The characters who mark transition points in God's saving acts have common traits. Zacharias and Elisabeth were devout, as were Simeon and Anna. The seven had notably devout natures. The centurion whose servant was healed showed the same kind of character (Luke 7:2-10). Now we meet Cornelius, a Gentile of spiritual and godly persuasion (Acts 10:1, 2).

"He was a man of wealth and noble birth, and his position was one of trust and honor. A heathen by birth, training, and education, through contact with the Jews he had gained a knowledge of God, and he worshiped Him with a true heart, showing the sincerity of his faith by compassion to the poor. . . . He had erected the altar of God in his home, for he dared not attempt to carry out his plans or to bear his responsibilities without the help of God." [2]

Herod the Great built Caesarea on the site of the Tower of Strato, northwest of Jerusalem, and named the town after the emperor. The Roman proconsul governed from there. Here lived Cornelius, captain of a group called the Italian band (verse 1). Cornelius was a popular name because it was the family name of Sulla, who had freed thousands of slaves.

Luke speaks of Cornelius's piety in verses 2, 4, 22, 30. "Here the idea is that the community does not accept just *any* Gentile, but only Gentiles of such piety that even a Jew must approve—and prayer and alms are (with fasting) *the* good works of Jewry. That an angel should come to such a man is perfectly comprehensible." [3]

Many Romans found Judaism attractive. Its monotheism and strict moral code contrasted sharply with polytheism and pagan laxity. Some made a complete change to Judaism. Others adhered to its moral principles and worshiped the one God. Christianity offered them salvation without the peculiar customs of the Law or Jewish exclusiveness.

Meanwhile, back at Simon's house Peter went up on the roof to pray (verse 9). The vision startled and baffled Peter. How could he have a vision from a divine source that commanded him to do what his religion forbade?

What should we conclude from the experience? Did the command to kill and eat (verse 13) do away with the age-old distinction between clean and unclean? Not at all.

Pollution by association had developed into a major concern of contemporary Judaism. Applied to food laws, it had come to mean that when clean animals came in contact with unclean animals, the clean were contaminated.

The animals in the sheet (verse 12) contained a hideous (to the devout Israelite) mixture of the clean and the unclean. Thus Peter saw no animal that he could kill and eat, because of the intermingling. Yet the Lord commanded just that.

The Lord's rebuke (verse 15) stressed a distinction. Peter should not call clean animals profane or common just because of association. He should discern according to the divine pattern. When the clean presented itself, he should take it as God's gift and not hesitate to eat.

Contact with Gentiles would not make Peter or any other Christian unclean. A Christian community with both Gentiles and Jews is not an unholy mixture of the chosen and the unacceptable. God calls all to Him, and the church, unlike too many in Judaism, must welcome freely all who trust in Jesus. Later Peter had problems

TIG-4

over eating with Gentiles (Gal. 2:11, 12). His vision should have kept him from such discriminatory actions.

Peter demonstrated his new view of mankind by his actions before he revealed his vision. The apostle raised no barriers against Gentiles (Acts 10:23). Later, refusing any special acknowledgment of his authority (verses 25, 26), he chatted with Cornelius (verse 27). Quite suddenly Peter stood alone in a room crowded with Gentiles (verse 27). Before ever he knew that Cornelius would accept the Lord, he made two of the most important pronouncements in the history of Christianity.

1. When devout persons present themselves in faith, their faith in God makes them as equally acceptable to the Christian community as a Jew. They are "clean" and worthy of acceptance.

2. Gentile associations pollute neither the God-fearing Gentile nor the Christian Jew. The gospel can go from all to all.

Peter declared God's openness to all human need (verse 34). Jesus Christ brought peace (verse 36; cf. Luke 2:14) to all men, thus conferring on all a privilege once open only to the believing Israelite. Jesus is Lord of all (verse 36), and everyone who trusts in Him will receive forgiveness of sin in His name (verse 42).

The apostle's proclamation about Jesus (verses 37-43) has a formal tone to it. It is something that a witnessing church member might use to declare himself, or a new convert might employ to speak to the accepting congregation.

The points are clear: (1) God's anointing of Jesus (verse 38); (2) Jesus' power and Spirit-filled life (verse 38); (3) His good deeds showing God's presence with Him (verse 38); (4) His crucifixion (verse 39); (5) the Resurrection (verse 40); (6) the command to witness (verse 41); (7) the coming judgment by Jesus Christ (verse 42); (8) the appeal, therefore, to turn to Him for forgiveness through trust in Him (verse 43).

The sequence of Pentecost repeated itself; devout people in prayer, awaiting God's action (verse 44). The crowd in the centurion's home (verse 24) paralleled that of the upper room. The conditions were ripe for another Spirit-inspired event.

Now followed the Pentecost of the Gentile world!

The Free Spirit at Work
Acts 10:44-11:18

Peter had just declared that the name of Jesus availed for everyone who trusted in Him (verse 43). We already know that it brings healing (Acts 3:16), that it represents the only name given for man's salvation (Acts 4:12). Jesus lives with His Father in heaven (Acts 7:55, 56); and has sent the Holy Spirit to His disciples (Acts 2:33).

But can the Spirit, always the special possession of God's people, transcend the barrier of the chosen people and fall on Gentiles? To the amazement of the Jewish Christians (Acts 10:45), He did just that.

Acts inseparably links trust in Jesus with the giving of the Holy Spirit. If the gospel is for all who believe, then through Jesus' name the Spirit will come to Gentiles as well as Jews. This moment in the Gentile home of Cornelius equals in significance any other Spirit-inspired event in Acts. The Spirit, who represented the hope of Israel for divine favor, now became a sign of the hope of all nations.

The gift included speaking in tongues. Again, this differs from the Corinthian gift for the following reasons: 1. Up to this point no record exists of anything except the gift of distinguishable languages as revealed at Pentecost. Anything other than that would puzzle the Christian Jews. 2. The gift was as "at the beginning" (Acts 11:15). 3. The gift of tongues included acclaiming God in an understandable way (Acts 10:46). 4. The Holy Spirit gave them no less a gift than the apostles themselves had received when they trusted Jesus for salvation (Acts

11:17).

The Spirit runs before us, opening doors we thought closed or making doors through walls we thought impenetrable. Precisely that very thing happened in Jerusalem.

Jewish Christians could accept that a proselyte to Judaism might later become a Christian (Acts 6:5). But Cornelius's faith had not been channeled through Judaism. Rather, it had flowed straight from him to Jesus Christ.

"They do not enter by way of the old Israel, for she stands under condemnation and, like the rest of mankind, has need of repentance (Acts 2:38; 3:19; 13:46), but what they enter is Israel renewed and restored (Acts 15:14, 16, 17), Israel whose Temple and circumcision are no longer the final signs of God's favor since they have been superseded by the Christ." [4]

Although Peter's vision had concerned *what* one might eat, the leaders in Jerusalem were more upset by *whom* Peter had eaten with (Acts 11:3).

The significance of table fellowship dominates associations in the writings of Luke. Jesus ate with sinners (Luke 15:1, 2). He set the precedent for the relaxed attitude of Peter. For the leaders at Jerusalem the matter had grave consequences. Were it known that the Christian community ate with Gentiles, and received them in spiritual fellowship with rather lax controls (in Jewish eyes), the whole security of the movement in Judea would be at risk.

The apostles thought that Peter might not be following God's way (Acts 11:17). But once the proof of God's presence and guidance comes, we should, like them, join in going His way (verse 18).

Some ancient manuscripts state that Peter stayed on in the area of Caesarea and did much preaching. Probably he established the first communities of Christian Gentiles in the history of the church. They would have developed a Christian life of their own, though most likely in association with Jewish Christians of the area.

Divine Grace at Work
Acts 11:18-30

In destroying Jewish categories for those who comprised God's elect, the church met new issues immediately. Not only Peter had success with Gentiles. While some spread the gospel only to Jews (Acts 11:19), others found interest among Gentiles (verse 20). A great many "Grecians" turned to the Lord as evangelists from Cyprus and Cyrene witnessed to them.

Syrian Antioch stood on the Orontes River. Rome made it the capital of the East, and the imperial legate governed from there. Most of the people were Syrians, but Jews formed a large community. A few miles out of town the groves of Daphne boasted the headquarters of the cult of Apollo and Artemis, infamous for moral debauchery. In the fourth and fifth decades A.D. the center of Christian missions shifted from Jerusalem to Antioch.

Again Barnabas, a man of rare charm and character, entered to play his role (verses 22-24). Barnabas always saw good in others. Possessing superior Christian graces, he could approach others without jealousy and was ready to excuse their faults, ready to help make peace.

In Antioch he consolidated and expanded the work of others (verse 24). Such men have always done the church good. The mixed group of Jews, God-fearing Gentiles, and former pagans that made up the Christian community in Antioch welded together under his influence.

Remembering Paul (verse 25), he went off to Tarsus to search him out and bring him back to Antioch as a fellow minister (verse 26). Barnabas's large spirit helped build men. He had no people file that excluded some from experiencing the power of the Spirit.

"It was in Antioch that the disciples were first called Christians. The name was given them because Christ was the main theme of their preaching, their teaching, and their conversation." [5]

The character of Barnabas showed in the organized response to Agabus's prophecy (verse 28). The disaster and famine relief offering in the church at Antioch had his support and sponsorship (verses 29, 30).

"The Lord in His wisdom has arranged that by means of the close relationship that should be maintained by all believers, Christian shall be united to Christian and church to church. Thus the human instrumentality will be enabled to cooperate with the divine. Every agency will be subordinate to the Holy Spirit, and all the believers will be united in an organized and well-directed effort to give to the world the glad tidings of the grace of God." [6]

---

[1] John Oxenham, "In Christ There Is No East Nor West," *The SDA Hymnal,* No. 587.

[2] White, *The Acts of the Apostles,* pp. 132, 133.

[3] Ernst Haenchen, *Acts of the Apostles,* pp. 357, 358.

[4] Eric Franklin, *Christ the Lord,* p. 125.

[5] White, *The Acts of the Apostles,* p. 157.

[6] *Ibid.,* p. 164.

Breaking
New Ground

Acts 12:1-13:52

The island of Mindanao in the south Philippines has harbored rebel fighters for more than a decade. They have attacked both political and religious figures. As many as 100 Seventh-day Adventists have died in the conflict.

In one recent incident an armed rebel commando abducted an Adventist preacher. When they blindfolded him and threatened execution, he protested that he was a pastor and not involved politically.

His claim had a familiar sound to the rebels. People often said they were priests or pastors when caught. But at the last moment the rebel captain relented long enough to order the prisoner to begin quoting texts on the Sabbath. One by one the pastor recited Bible passages, explaining their meaning. Finally the captain confessed quietly to the pastor that he had had an Adventist upbringing. Eventually they let him go.

Such episodes illustrate two aspects of Acts 12: God does deliver, but not everyone escapes; and arrogant power has its day of reckoning with God.

Tyrants and the Faithful
Acts 12:1, 2

Ancient Israel had known despotic power. Daniel used the Babylonian model of cruel persecution and religious tyranny to describe all religiopolitical combinations. In the Gospels and Acts the puppet rulers of Rome demonstrated the same cruelty as Babylon. The Herod family especially ranged itself against God's will.

1. Herod the Great ruled Judea and Palestine at the time of Jesus' birth. Though an Edomite, he was a Jew by citizenship and religious practice. He rebuilt Zerubbabel's Temple, and constructed a palace in Jerusalem. Later he sought to murder the infant Jesus (Matt. 2:1-18).

2. Archelaus, a son of Herod the Great, governed Judea, Samaria, and Idumea. In order to escape a possible threat from him, Joseph and Mary went to live in Nazareth after their return from Egypt (Matt. 2:22, 23). He ruled by violence, like his father.

3. Herod Antipas, called the Herod the Tetrarch, controlled Galilee and Perea during Jesus' ministry. A brother of Archelaus, he achieved notoriety by stealing his niece, Herodias, who was married to his half brother Herod Philip. When John rebuked Herod Antipas for his adultery, Herodias had the Baptist executed (Matt. 14:1-12). Antipas lived as an orthodox Jew. On one of his visits to Jerusalem for the feast of Passover, Pilate sought his friendship by sending Jesus to him (Luke 23:8-12).

Now Herod Agrippa I appears. King of all Judea and Palestine, he persecuted the apostles (Acts 12:1), executing James, the son of Zebedee (verse 2). Later two of his daughters, Bernice and Drusilla, are mentioned in Luke's story. His son Herod Agrippa II participated in the dispatch of Paul to Rome.

The cynical use of power by the Herods affected the Christian movement. However, persecution and murder also forced the Christian leaders away from the use of political influence as a way of achieving their mission. In this they differed sharply from the leaders of the Jews. In later centuries Christian leaders forgot the lessons of the early years and sought political power.

Prayer Has Its Answer
Acts 12:3-25

Herod Agrippa I planned to execute Peter also (Acts

12:3), hoping thereby to gain the support of the religious rulers (verse 3). Because Peter had escaped once before (Acts 5:19), Herod tried to prevent his getting away again (Acts 12:4).

But who can resist the power of God (verse 5)? In trying to thwart God's will Herod opened an opportunity for the church. As a result of his violent actions the church would find itself relying more and more on God's power.

Peter faced death in confidence. "Since his reinstatement after his denial of Christ, he had unflinchingly braved danger, and had shown a noble courage and boldness in preaching a crucified, risen, and ascended Saviour. . . . Peter believed that the time had come for him to yield up his life for Christ's sake." [1]

How often God answers our prayers while we are praying them (verse 7)! Intercessory prayer places us in the position where God can act on our behalf.

"The most difficult prayer, and the prayer which, therefore, costs us the most striving, is persevering prayer, the prayer which faints not, but continues steadfastly until the answer comes. To strive in prayer for a person or for a cause means, in the first place, to live, feel, and suffer with that person or for that cause. . . . In the second place, to strive in prayer means to struggle through those hindrances which would restrain or even prevent us entirely from continuing in persevering prayer." [2]

Luke relishes a good story and tells this one with detail and color. The maximum-security prison confined Peter within three distinct doors or gates (verse 10). Manacles handcuffed him to two soldiers, while sentries guarded the cell (verse 6).

Release began with the prayer of the people (verse 5). Neither the light, the urgent command of the angel, the clank of the falling chains, nor the opening and closing of gates woke the wardens (verses 7, 10). If Peter thought it a vision (verse 9), his captors may have thought it a dream.

Rhoda ("Rose") recognized the apostle's voice, but in her joy failed to open the door for him (verses 13, 14). Anyone who experienced this event would never forget that little episode, and later might have had a chuckle over it. Peter made short work of his explanations (verse 17). Remembering Paul's narrow escape over the wall of Damascus, Peter thought discretion the better part of valor, and slipped away to an unrevealed destination. But not to Rome, for in chapter 15 we shall meet him again in Jerusalem.

The Roman Catholic Church has claimed that Peter went to Rome at an early date and worked there for about 30 years. No evidence exists to support the idea, though he did spend time in Rome and died there.

James, a valued and beloved leader, died, while Peter, an equally loved and valued leader, lived. Why? God worked through the disaster to accomplish His will. So often Satan seeks to frustrate the plans of God. But for each land mine Satan plants in the path of God's people, the Lord builds a new road to the future.

But what of Herod, the "devil's finger"? In typical fashion he vented his anger on the luckless guards (verse 19). Time passed. His success with the Jews, because of James's execution, made him attempt one more grand deed.

Josephus says that Herod's flatterers said, "Be gracious to us, if hitherto we have reverenced thee as a human being, yet henceforth we acknowledge thee to be of more than human nature."

The ruler failed to honor God (verses 21, 22). One day his silver garments flashed in the sun in a blinding display of pomp and pride. The next day he was dying a hideous death (verse 23). According to Josephus, it took him five days to die.

The most likely cause of death was the bursting of an hydatid cyst, an extremely painful and revolting demise.

The angel from the Lord struck him down (verse 23), declaring God's judgment against all who usurp His name and destroy His saints (Dan. 7:26, 27). Projected into the cosmic realm, James's death, Peter's escape, and Herod's elimination give a similar picture to the broader visions of the Apocalypse.

Breaking New Ground for the Gospel
Acts 13:1-52

The first missionary journey of Paul took about three years. The church at Antioch commissioned and supported the endeavor (Acts 13:4). Paul, Barnabas, and their assistant, John Mark (verse 5; cf. Acts 12:12), worked to provide their living, a common practice in both Jewish and early Christian missionary activity.

The prophets and teachers listed (Acts 13:1) show the wide appeal of the Christian gospel. Barnabas, a Jew, came from Cyprus; Lucius, from Cyrene in North Africa; Simeon may have been called Niger because of Negro ancestry; Manaen, a courtier from Herod's establishment, had aristocratic connections; and Paul, from Tarsus in Asia Minor, had rabbinic training. Already we are seeing the amazing ability of the gospel to create and hold together its own "United Nations."

"John Mark was with them as their helper *(hyperetes)*. Jewish inscriptions and various papyri use the word *hyperetes* in the sense of a synagogue attendant, as does Luke also in his Gospel (4:20). This has caused many to view John Mark's responsibilities within the missionary party as related to caring for the scrolls (the Scriptures), together with a possible 'Sayings of Jesus' collection and serving as a catechist for new converts." [3]

Saul (Acts 13:9) had at least four names. Among Jews he proudly bore the name of Israel's first king. As a Roman citizen he would have had at least two Roman names, a *praenomen* and a *nomen,* though we do not know what they were. As a Jew from the Diaspora he also bore the

Greek name Paulus, by which the world, then as now, came to know him.

Sergius Paulus of Paphos (verse 7) appears to have been the procurator of Cyprus during the time of Claudius. He asked the evangelists to appear before him and explain their mission. In his court Bar-Jesus, or Elymas, had set himself up as spokesman for the Hebrew faith.

In strong, biblical terms Paul condemned the sorcery of Elymas (verses 10, 11). Earlier Peter had met a similar danger with equally drastic action (Acts 8:20-22). The effect of such miracles helped to advance the cause of Christ (Acts 13:12).

"[Mark] was disheartened by the perils and privations of the way. He had labored with success under favorable circumstances; but now, amidst the opposition and perils that so often beset the pioneer worker, he failed to endure hardness as a good soldier of the cross. . . . As the apostles advanced, and still greater difficulties were apprehended, Mark was intimidated and, losing all courage, refused to go farther and returned to Jerusalem" [4]

After the long march from Perga to Pisidian Antioch the apostles went straight to the synagogue (verse 14). "In the first century A.D. the synagogue service comprised the Sh'ma, the prayer (of 18 petitions) and priestly blessing, then reading (in vernacular translation) from the law and—though not at every service—the prophets; next followed a free address, usually exhortatory, which the leader could invite any competent Jew to deliver." [5]

While we do not have all that Paul said, we are hearing the essentials of Paul's missionary preaching to Jews and God-fearers (verse 26).

The essentials are: (1) God's choice of Israel (verse 17); (2) His power and perseverance (verses 17, 18); (3) the Davidic promises (verses 22, 23); (4) the preaching of John the Baptist (verses 24, 25); (5) the failure of the Jerusalem

Jews to acknowledge Jesus, the Saviour (verses 23, 26, 27); (6) the unjust execution of Jesus, the Messiah (verses 27-29); (7) the resurrection of Jesus (verses 30, 31); (8) how the good news about Jesus affects faith (verse 38); (9) the justification of sinners (verse 39); and (10) a warning about the results of rejecting Jesus (verses 40, 41).

The four-point Christian confession of Acts 13:28-31 echoes 1 Corinthians 15:3-5: (1) the Crucifixion (Acts 13:28, 29); (2) He was laid in a tomb (verse 29); (3) "God raised him from the dead" (verse 30); and (4) "for many days he was seen by those who had traveled with him from Galilee to Jerusalem," and were now His witnesses (verse 31, NIV).

Psalm 2:7 declares Messiah (and thus Jesus) to be the Son of God, begotten of the Father (Acts 13:33). Paul put the verse alongside 2 Samuel 7:6-16 (verse 34; cf. Isa. 55:3). The community at Qumran (the people of the Dead Sea scrolls) had already linked these passages and applied them to the Messiah. By uniting these verses, Paul joined Old Testament redemptive history and the history of Jesus. What happened to Jesus was truly Messianic, and fulfilled Israel's expectations (Acts 13:35).

There can be no doubt that Paul made an effective and persuasive presentation of the gospel, arguing in Jewish terms in such a way that they would see Jesus as the Promised One and put their trust in Him (verses 38, 39). Many parallels exist between Paul's sermon and Peter's sermons in Acts 2-4.

"We should bear in mind (a) Paul's own insistence that the gospel story which he proclaimed was the same as that proclaimed by the other apostles (1 Cor. 15:11), (b) the fact that the common outline of the apostolic *kerygma* may be traced throughout the whole NT, no matter who the writer or speaker may be, (c) the evidence for a 'testimony' collection used by all the early preachers of the gospel, which goes far to account for the common interdependent exegesis of OT passages." [6]

What does Paul mean by *justify* (Acts 13:39)? Is Paul proposing a works-plus-Christ justification in Acts? Not at all. Rather, Paul is declaring the complete justifying grace of Christ, which found no counterpart in the Law of Moses.

The quote from Habakkuk 1:5 (verse 41) reinforces his interpretation. What Paul proposed brought an unheard-of deed from God—justification in Christ. Repudiating the Law as a means of being right with God was no small matter for a devout Jew. If Paul could find support in the Prophets, they might accept his appeal.

One can imagine the scene next Sabbath (verse 44). Paul and Barnabas had continued private discussions with many (verse 43) and the apostle urged on them the grace of God in contrast to the Law of Moses.

But not only the Jews and their proselytes (verse 43) wanted to hear him further on the matter. That Sabbath the whole city flooded into the streets to hear Paul (verse 44).

Free from pressure from Jerusalem, the local Jewish community might have accepted Jesus and spearheaded a mission to the surrounding cities and nations (verse 46). But it was not to be.

God had intended that Israel should be a light to the Gentiles (verse 47). If the synagogues would not fulfill that purpose, then the church must.

Paul did not preach predestination (verse 48). Later Luke records the working of the Spirit in the life of a convicted person (Acts 16:14). Conversion had nothing automatic or ordained about it. Every city contained some who were God's people (Acts 18:10). Acts 13:48 records the results of the preaching of Paul, rather than the gathering to the church of predetermined individuals.

The opposition now encountered (verse 50) became a pattern in the Pauline missionary travels. Such a stir would arise in each place that the Romans would note it, and the apostles would have to leave because of the leverage the Jews could apply against officials.

"It was customary for Jews to 'shake off the dust' of a pagan town 'from their feet' when they returned to their own land. . . . The Christians were demonstrating in a particularly vigorous manner that Jews who rejected the gospel and drove out the missionaries were no longer truly part of Israel but were no better than unbelievers." [7]

In all this we see portents of great things to come. The joy and the Holy Spirit that permeated the early believers (verse 52) also fills all who serve the Lord today. Not just the grace of God or the acquittal from the guilt of our sins, brings joy, but also—and perhaps even more important—we rejoice as the Spirit leads others to our Lord.

[1] *The SDA Bible Commentary*, Ellen G. White Comments, vol. 6, p. 1061.

[2] O. Hallesby, *Prayer*, p. 88.

[3] Gaebelein, ed., *The Expositor's Bible Commentary*, vol. 9, p. 419.

[4] White, *The Acts of the Apostles*, pp. 169, 170.

[5] Haenchen, *Acts of the Apostles*, pp. 407, 408.

[6] F. F. Bruce, *The Book of the Acts*, p. 277.

[7] I .Howard Marshall, *Acts: An Introduction and Commentary*, p. 231.

Faith Active in Love

Acts 14:1-15:35

If the Spirit truly is the in-between God, then He will work within the church to resolve issues and maintain Christian charity and love. As you read Galatians you will recognize the intensity of the battle of words and actions that raged over the issue of obedience to the Law of Moses. Was it all done in love? Probably not.

As Paul summed it up, faith active in love (Gal. 5:6) counted far more than strict obedience to ceremony and sacrifice. Faith that worked through love would truly produce the new creature (Gal. 6:15). And who would do this among God's people? "The harvest of the Spirit is love . . . If the Spirit is the source of our life, let the Spirit also direct our course" (Gal. 5:22, 25, NEB).

In the mountains of West Virginia I watched two mighty warriors in the faith cross swords over an issue much like the one the church faced in the time of Paul. How should we regard righteousness by faith? What will it bring to fruit in our lives? The words grew in strength, adjectives attached themselves to them, the pronouns turned from *we* and *they* to *you* and *your* as accusations flew.

Then, quite suddenly, something happened, as the senior church statesman intervened. Redemptive processes took over. Reconcile, the Spirit was saying. And He brought just that to pass. Out of the reconciliation came strength for us—a sounder position, a joy in the Spirit's guidance (Acts 13:52).

Persuasion and Persecution
Acts 14:1-28

A pattern now developed in the church's advance. Paul or another Christian missionary would preach in the synagogue on successive Sabbaths for as long as possible, resulting in many Jews and Gentile God-fearers deciding for Christ (Acts 14:1). Those Jews who would not accept Jesus now forced the apostles away from the synagogue (verse 2). Evangelism then moved to other places where the crowds would grow even larger (verse 3). Finally the Jews would use political influence to force the preachers to flee (verses 4, 5).

The conflict between Paul and the Jews asked the question that the council in Jerusalem finally answered: Were the Christians wrong in urging Jesus Christ as the sole means of salvation? And when Gentiles accept Jesus, how should they show their faith?

The poison of slander and misrepresentation did not work at first in Iconium (verses 2, 3). While those Jews who rejected Jesus as Messiah were persuading the Gentiles to join them against the apostles, Paul and Barnabas used the time to good advantage, establishing the new converts and adding to their number (verse 3).

"Often, by misrepresentation and falsehood, the enemies of the gospel have seemingly triumphed, closing the doors by which God's messengers might gain access to the people. But these doors cannot remain forever closed, and often, as God's servants have returned after a time to resume their labors, the Lord has wrought mightily in their behalf, enabling them to establish memorials to the glory of His name." [1]

The early church found that growth can be painful (verse 5). Like the church, the Christian must also learn that lesson. Victorious living, bold faith, consistent witness—these do not always arrive ready-made, but have to be struggled for against opposition.

Luke speaks of Paul and Barnabas as apostles (verses 4, 14), the only place in Acts where anyone except the twelve have that title. Paul used the words as a general term for those sent on missionary work (Eph. 4:11).

More than once, the Christian movement had friends in the councils of their enemies that enabled the missionaries to escape (Acts 14:5, 6). From Iconium Paul and Barnabas went to the region of Lystra and Derbe, also working in the villages and farms of the area (verses 6, 7).

The author of Acts employs his storyteller's skill to add local color and detail to the miracle at Lystra (verses 8, 9), a style of writing that is characteristic of him. One passage will be spare and almost dry in approach, then he will enliven the record with action verbs and vivid detail (verses 10, 11).

Greatly impressed with the miraculous healing, the people referred respectfully to Paul as Mercury and to Barnabas as Jupiter (verse 12). According to Roman mythology, Jupiter ruled the assembly of gods and Mercury was his spokesman. Their Greek names were Zeus and Hermes, respectively. A common belief held that gods in human form and garb might show up unannounced.

"The people around Lystra told a story that once Zeus and Hermes had come to this earth in disguise. None in all the land would give them hospitality until at last two old peasants, Philemon and his wife, Baucis, took them in. As a result the whole population was wiped out by the gods except Philemon and Baucis, who were made guardians of a splendid temple and were turned into two great trees when they died." [2]

Paul and Barnabas could not understand the local language. As the oxen and garlands moved with the crowds toward the temple outside the gate, the apostles suddenly realized that they were the target of worship (verse 14).

Their brief speech (verses 15-17) may represent the

typical approach of both Christians and Jews to pagan audiences. With the question of superstitious belief settled (verse 15)—at least in the apostles' minds—the two proceeded to declare "the living God" (verse 15) the Creator of all. Paul uses a similar approach in Athens (Acts 17:22-31) where his chief listeners were Athenian philosophers. To the Thessalonians he wrote along the same lines (1 Thess. 1:9).

The apostle taught that the Creator provided evidence of His existence and His care (Acts 15:16, 17). In Romans 1:19, 20 he argued for a universal knowledge of God. But he did not stop there. In his evangelism he followed that approach with the gospel, declaring how Jesus, the Son of God, brings salvation. Paul preached of the God who created and who provides. He did not teach that God is a part of the natural world. Pantheism had no appeal to Jewish or Christian minds.

His audience was entirely pagan—the first such occasion, and a most significant one in the story of the early church. But the Jews had now begun to track Paul and Barnabas, and finally caught up with the apostles in the midst of their missionary activities (Acts 14:19). Paul recorded the trials experienced at Antioch, Iconium, and Lystra (2 Tim. 3:10, 11). He tells how the Lord rescued him and will also keep those who trust Him secure from the distressing effects of persecution (verses 12, 13).

The victories of Lystra almost ended in disaster. An incensed crowd now turned on Paul, the spokesman (Acts 14:19). It would have taken only a few words to twist what he had said to mean an attack on the local gods, and especially on Zeus.

The event at Lystra echoes the stoning of Stephen (verse 19). Both were lynchings that came at the climax of a powerful presentation overthrowing the existing view of religious belief. Stephen infuriated the Sanhedrin by declaring their faith and their Temple purposeless. Paul enraged the Lystran Gentiles by denying the existence of

Zeus and Hermes and calling them no more than idols. Thus Paul too felt the suffering that Jesus had told him would come (Acts 9:16).

The elders that the apostles ordained (Acts 14:23) would have approximated in function those of a Jewish synagogue. A similar group of officers governed the church at Antioch.

Two pictures of ministry emerge from Acts, but not necessarily mutually exclusive. Both may have flourished, even within the same congregation. The first places the twelve in authority over the whole church. To them the Spirit adds the seven in a secondary administrative and evangelistic role. Elders appear in Acts 11:30 and again in Acts 14:23. They share authority with the apostles (Acts 15:2, 4).

Ordination (Acts 14:23) separated the elders for their specific responsibility. Though the office of elder was sacred, it did not give the holder a monopoly on the Spirit or any one of His gifts. The Spirit operated both through organization (Acts 13:2) and through individuals not always in touch with central authority (Acts 8:26, 39).

The apostles Paul and Barnabas did not return to Antioch to report on structure! They came to tell how God had given a great harvest of souls as a reward for their ministry and the faith of the Antioch church in sponsoring the endeavor.

What Stephen had so clearly foreseen, what the Lord Himself had promised, what Peter had urged, was now coming true. God would go with His messengers wherever they went (Acts 14:27). The Son of man knew no restrictions in the sending of the Spirit.

The Spirit moves among us, guiding and directing. Organizer, motivator, ordainer of men and women to His work, He is never far from us. Yet as Acts says again and again, He ever moves, and best moves, through those who place their trust in Jesus and submit to His will.

Freedom, Law, and Lifestyle
Acts 15:1-35

If the Spirit would guide the young church into unity, then He must now face its most critical test. From the distance of the twentieth century, the issues seem alien, almost bizarre. Who today must test his faith against meat offered to idols? And where in the civilized world are we close enough to the slaughtering of animals to know whether the beast was strangled or dispatched some other way? Only on the question of morality do we find common ground.

One single, verifiable physical modification distinguished the Jewish male from his Gentile counterpart. Circumcision had an overwhelming religious and national importance to the Jews. It originated with Abraham, Moses had enshrined it in the Law, and the scribes had given it theological value.

The claim (Acts 15:1) that Gentiles must also undergo circumcision seemed natural enough. The reasoning went like this. God has chosen Israel. Circumcision is the sign by which one acknowledges that choice. Christianity is the new Israel. God is giving all the Old Testament blessings to the new Israel. All who enter that new Israel must be circumcised.

The council had to distinguish between Jewish traditions and God's new revelation in Jesus. The church's leaders must have wondered what the effect of any decisions would be on the leaders of Judaism, and even more on the Gentiles.

This key chapter of Acts asks still other questions: "Does the Lord speak through one single office-bearer, through a governing body, through the church meeting? ... The church as a whole shares in the authority of Jesus Christ. Again the New Testament is unanimous that regard must be had to the whole body of members." [3]

In Acts 14 we read of elders appointed in the churches. Such elders themselves became representatives in wider councils of the church (Acts 15:4). The congregation at Antioch sent Paul on his way (verse 2) to speak for them in Jerusalem. The church supported the consensus over the Law (verse 22). Any major decision must involve the whole of the church with all of its many units.

The council convened under considerable tension (verse 2). We do not know how many of the twelve apostles were present. Now James, the brother of the Lord and not of the twelve, and Peter, when present from his own mission, exercised leadership positions. Apparently because of his skill, and because he stayed put in Jerusalem, James had the principal role at this point.

When James ended the discussion it had the support of the apostles and elders (verse 22). In fact, the whole church agreed. It is almost beyond belief that such intensely nationalistic Hebrews could open the door to the new Israel as wide as they did. A radical decision such as this did not come easily as Galatians 1 and 2 make clear.

Peter's speech reveals the following early Christian attitudes: 1. God chose from among the apostles and elders those who would carry the gospel to the Gentiles. Peter was one such, as were also Paul and Barnabas (Acts 15:7, 12). 2. The gift of the Holy Spirit, rather than circumcision or any other outward sign, showed that God had approved the response of faith (verse 8). 3. God does not respect the person of the Jew above the Gentile. The lives of the Gentile converts showed the same purity of lifestyle that a Jewish Christian was expected to show (verse 9). 4. Faith rather than conformity to the Law brought salvation (verse 9).

The council emphasized the need for an appropriate lifestyle. Christian freedom was never intended to produce immorality or negligence of the Ten Commandments.

Paul and Barnabas had rapt attention as they told the exciting story of evangelism among the Gentiles (verse 12). With them were Gentile representatives from the Antioch church, who showed that faith in Jesus could govern the way a person lived far more effectively than ceremony or a strict legal code.

James's speech shifted the discussion from the saving of the Gentiles to the end-time. The prophets had predicted that the Gentiles would be with the remnant of Israel in the restoration of "David's fallen tent" (verses 16-18, NIV). Among the Jewish Christians present, James's argument may actually have been as compelling as those of Peter or Paul. The fulfillment of the prophetic messages had dominated Christianity's beginnings. But they could only be completely fulfilled through the inclusion of Gentile Christians; therefore, the church must not only welcome such a development, but make it a chief concern. The end-time argument of James shows how much the church depended on fulfilled prophecy in understanding its mission.

The mix of presentations—Peter with his emphasis on Cornelius's conversion, Paul and Barnabas with their stories of great success, and the theology of James—all brought unity (verse 22).

The actual decree (verses 28, 29) leaves out so many things that one can only assume that they were commonly accepted practice and not under dispute. Not mentioned were baptism, the Lord's Supper, the Ten Commandments (except fornication), the Sabbath—even the gift of the Spirit has no mention. Rather, the decree says what not to do.

We have no reason to doubt Luke's assessment (verse 28) that the Holy Spirit guided the council to a peaceable and far-ranging decision that began then to take hold of church attitudes and theology. "The Holy Spirit saw good not to impose the ceremonial law on the Gentile converts, and the mind of the apostles regarding this matter was as the mind of the Spirit of God." [4]

The requirements placed on Gentile Christians aided them in avoiding that which was particularly offensive to Jews. The emphasis on food laws indicates that questions of clean and unclean foods were prominent. We should understand the decree in light of Acts 10 and 11, where the vision given Peter maintained the distinction between clean and unclean foods but excluded the belief that clean meats might become polluted through association.

Back at home base in Antioch Paul and Barnabas once more resumed their evangelistic role (Acts 15:35). The reports from the Jerusalem Council encouraged and strengthened the faith of the believers (verses 30, 31). The church viewed this amicable solution as one possible only through the working of the Spirit.

The Jerusalem Council (1) rejected the Law of Moses as a means of salvation; (2) permitted Hebrew Christians to obey national traditions without embarrassment or compromise; and (3) established a procedure for settling significant differences within the church. Later Paul would declare the instruction about meat offered to idols, strangled animals, and the use of blood irrelevant in relation to salvation (1 Cor. 10:19-26). He also urged that our actions not offend others.

"Paul and Barnabas left the convention feeling just the way we do when we leave our conventions. How slowly they seem to move! How they seem to resist the Holy Spirit! How afraid they are to take a brave, daring stand! And yet looking back on them all, beginning with this one in Jerusalem, we see that God moves slowly but surely through their cautious and often clumsy movements." [5]

---

[1] White, *The Acts of the Apostles*, p. 179.
[2] William Barclay, *The Acts of the Apostles*, p. 109.
[3] Schweizer, *Church Order in the New Testament*, p. 190.
[4] White, *The Acts of the Apostles*, p. 194.
[5] *The Interpreter's Bible*, vol. 9, p. 208.

Poses, Prejudice, and Philosophy

Acts 15:36-17:34

How often prejudice and preconceived notions cloud our judgment! I remember a meeting that discussed the fate of one of our valued administrators. Had his effectiveness ended? Should the church dismiss him?

Senior employees recounted problems that had arisen during his leadership. One man cited the individual's penchant for traveling. But from a management viewpoint his work had proved that he could make economies and put the institution on a track toward greater efficiency.

In the end we found another assignment for the man. Today he continues as a senior and respected manager of a large enterprise run by the church. A few words might have pushed him out. With a little counsel and a new start he has continued to serve.

In 1 Corinthians 12-14 Paul recounts the tensions that he found in that church. He asks it to understand what is happening when good people, devoted to Christ, have differing interests and approaches. In such diversity the eye of faith discerns the Holy Spirit at work. He is providing for the church the very diversity that it needs to meet the challenge of witness.

Luke chronicles the early church, warts and all. He recounts Paul and Barnabas's dispute over the fate of John Mark (Acts 15:36-39). Having high standards, Paul despised men who sought their own welfare rather than the Lord's (Phil. 2:20, 21). (Later he may have had more than one occasion to reflect on his judgmental attitude and temper [Acts 15:39; 23:3; cf. 1 Cor. 13:5; 2 Tim. 4:1].)

Luke records that the two men "departed asunder" (Acts 15:39), a verb used in only one other place in the New Testament; in Revelation 6:14 it describes the apocalyptic vision of the heavens departing like a scroll.

Although the matter was deemed serious enough to merit a separation at that point, Paul later found Mark a useful help (Col. 4:10; 2 Tim. 4:11). Having decided to split up the team from the first journey, Paul and Barnabas headed in different directions. While we hear no more of the work of the Barnabas-Mark team, through this parting the Spirit doubled the witnesses.

When the Spirit of Jesus Intervenes
Acts 15:36-16:40

Acts 15 begins with a demand from some Judeans that Gentiles be circumcised. The council rejected their demand. Chapter 16 opens with the circumcision of a half Gentile, Timothy, and Paul, of all people, saw to it that the rite was carried out. Furthermore, he did so while in the process of delivering the edict from the Jerusalem council (Acts 16:3, 4).

In the eyes of the Gentiles Timothy was as good as a Jew, having been brought up by a Jewish mother. Yet from a Jewish perspective he was no better than a Gentile unless circumcised (verse 1). More than once Paul showed himself ready for conciliation with Jewish opinion (Acts 21:26; cf. 1 Cor. 9:19-22).

"When Timothy was little more than a boy, Paul took him with him as his companion in labor. Those who had taught Timothy in his childhood were rewarded by seeing the son of their care linked in close fellowship with the great apostle." [1]

Scholars have differed vehemently where Paul went on the second journey (Acts 16:4-7). "Some have contended that Paul's Galatian churches, those to whom he addressed his letter, were in the north. . . . Ramsay's careful collection of epigraphical evidence has, however, satisfactorily proved that the recipients of the letter were the south Galatian churches and that Luke's geographical terminology was precise. . . . The demonstration that the Galatia of the New Testament was south Galatia made the theory of those critics who regarded the Acts of the Apostles as a late, apologetic fabrication no longer tenable. It stands proven that the Galatian passages could have been written only by a first-century historian who wrote naturally in the geographical terminology of contemporary inscriptions." [2]

The Spirit directed Paul and Silas to Europe (verse 9). Some scholars have suggested that the man in the vision may have been Luke himself. Luke waxed quite enthusiastic over Philippi (verse 12), making sure readers would know how important it was.

Philip, the father of Alexander the Great, had founded Philippi to dominate the trading routes of northern Greece. The plain around Philippi had a military importance like that of Megiddo in Palestine. Near Philippi the leadership of Rome was decided after the assassination of Julius Caesar. The city had a school of medicine (did Luke train there?).

Where no synagogue existed and when climate made it possible, the Jews of the Dispersion tended to meet by a river or the sea (Ps. 137). Lydia (Acts 16:13, 14) had been converted to Judaism in her hometown Thyatira. She extracted a reddish-purple dye from the madder root and sold cloth dyed with it.

Having journeyed from paganism to Judaism and then from Judaism to Christianity, Lydia evangelized both family and servants (Acts 16:15). She joins Dorcas and Martha as an example of hospitality.

During Jesus' ministry, people possessed with evil spirits shouted out derisively as He passed (Luke 4:34, 41). He exorcised them. And now Paul did the same for the bedeviled young woman in Philippi (Acts 16:18).

"Her gift is attributed by Luke to 'a spirit of divination,' literally 'a spirit, a python.' The latter word originally meant a snake, and in particular the snake which guarded the celebrated oracle at Delphi. . . . In the present case the girl presumably spoke like a ventriloquist and had the gift of clairvoyance; therefore Luke described her as having a spirit (i.e., an evil spirit), namely one capable of ventriloquism." [3]

Those who gained by duping the crowds stirred them up against the two Christians. A surging, yelling mob frequently dominates the action in Luke's record (verse 22). At times the Christian witness escapes, though with difficulty; at times he, like his Master, suffers their wrath.

"The charge laid was that Paul and Silas were advocating a *religio illicita* ["illegal religion"] and thus disturbing the Pax Romana. But the charge, being couched in terms that appealed to the latent anti-Semitism of the people ("these men are Jews") and their racial pride ("us Romans"), ignited the flames of bigotry and prejudice. . . . Timothy and Luke, however, being respectively half Jewish and fully Gentile . . . were left alone. Anti-Semitism lay very near the surface throughout the Roman Empire. Here it seems to have taken over not only in laying the charge but also in identifying the defendants." [4]

Now came a series of miracles:

1. The miracle of faith that enabled Paul and Silas to sing praises to God from the dungeon (verse 25). Years before, Jesus had said, "Rejoice when you are persecuted" (Matt. 5:11, 12; cf. Rom. 5:3; 1 Peter 5:6).

2. The miracle of the earthquake (Acts 16:26). The shackles would have been riveted into the wall. The rivets fell away, not just from Paul and Silas, but from all the prisoners.

3. The miracle of the prisoners who did not seek to escape (verse 28). The jailer nearly killed himself because

his life was forfeit if even one prisoner got away (verse 27).

4. The miracle of the converted jailer (verse 30).

5. The miracle of the humbled jailer (verse 33). How the life changes when Jesus enters!

6. The miracle of release without reason (verse 35).

7. The miracle of the fearless Paul (verses 37-39). His action gave legitimacy to the Christian church in Philippi and protected it from future molestation.

Reactions to the Word
Acts 17:1-34

The mission strategy of the great apostle bears some reflection. His activity at Thessalonica (Acts 17:1) is typical of it: go where the response will most likely be greatest (verse 2), then spread out after you have found a favorable reaction (verse 3).

The search for receptive communities, family groups, or individuals is important in any advance the church makes. Again and again we have proved that mission expands best through the networking of families, relatives, friendships, and clan groupings.

The suffering, death, and resurrection of the Messiah held a key role in convincing Jews to accept Christianity. Paul based his teaching on Scripture (verse 2), probably using such passages as Isaiah 53 and Psalm 110 to carry the thrust of the Christian appeal. Summed up, though, Paul's preaching said simply, "And this Jesus, . . . whom I am proclaiming to you, is the Messiah" (Acts 17:3, NEB).

On a previous occasion (Acts 13:50) women of standing incited by the Jews joined crowds opposing Paul and Barnabas. In Thessalonica women of influence converted to Christianity (Acts 17:4).

The women probably had little influence with the Jews. Paul recounts his own experience in Thessalonica (1 Thess. 2:15, 16). The Jews there treated him much as they did the Lord Jesus. First they rejected his appeals, then sought to destroy him. The Thessalonians themselves suffered at the hands of their fellow citizens as other Christians had (verses 13, 14).

Angry at the loss of the support of the God-fearing Gentiles, the Jews descended into the slums of the city, stirring up the unemployed and ignorant to attack Paul and Silas (verse 5). Jason was probably a Jewish convert who had adopted his name because it approximated Joshua (verse 6).

The church's enemies took a cunning approach (verses 7, 8). Roman history reveals the tragic end of a number of popular politicians. To eliminate them, their enemies accused them of plotting to take over the empire. The Christians, so it was said, planned to put Jesus on the throne. Even without any evidence this charge could have destroyed Paul and Silas.

The problem for the Christians was that the charge had just that tinge of truth that made it believable and threatening. Paul filled his preaching to the Thessalonians with references to the end time (1 Thess. 1:9, 10; 4:15-18; 2 Thess. 1:9, 10; 2). He would sound to the untutored ear as urging a radical change in the political system that would make Jesus king over all.

The magistrates reacted in a restrained way (Acts 17:9). They bound Jason over to keep the peace. Paul spoke of the hindrance of Satan, referring to his unexpected and urgent flight from the city (verse 10).

Reactions among the Jews varied. In Berea results were rapid and satisfying (verse 11). Luke continually refers to the influence of women who joined the church (verse 12). But Paul did not have long to remain in this receptive community (verse 13). Again the believers hustled him off, this time to Athens.

In Athens Paul launched a two-pronged mission. In the synagogue he argued from Scripture that Jesus was the Messiah, and he used his Gentile approach in street preaching (Acts 17:17).

The detached, laid-back citizens had seen and heard

it all (verses 18-21). They viewed Paul with some amusement—a novelty to help pass the time of day, but hardly someone to take seriously (verse 18).

During Paul's day Athens did not boast a great philosopher. However, it had schools of philosophy. Two of them, one based on Epicurus and the other on Zeno, had great popularity. Epicurus (342-270 B.C.) taught that the gods had no interest in man. Therefore he urged a life devoted to pleasure. The greatest pleasure came if one had no pain, stress, or tension. Zeno (335-265 B.C.) founded Stoicism, so-called because he taught in the *stoa*, a painted cloister in the *agora* (marketplace). Teaching self-sufficiency and urging his followers to follow reason, he thought of God as the world soul, a key concept in pantheism.

The street philosophers dubbed Paul a "babbler" (verse 18). In Greek the word originally applied to birds picking up grain, then to junk collectors, and finally to those who grabbed ideas from here and there.

Just what the listeners thought of Jesus and the resurrection (verse 18) is not certain. It appears that they may have considered Jesus a god and resurrection His consort.

Paul used the typical arguments of the Old Testament prophets (verses 24, 25). God Himself had given life and intelligence to the human who made the idols. Ought not man then bypass and reject the man-made for the One who made man?

The differences of tribe and nation, of language and color, did not demand a separate god for each. Such diversity is only superficial; all nations are "of one blood" (verse 26). As Creator God He has considered the time and place when and where each nation should receive the call to worship Him (verse 26).

Not that they should think that God has ignored them (against Epicureanism) (verse 27). Rather, He has always been near, sustaining all in a personal way (against

Stoicism) (verse 28).

Paul taught the unity of the human race. All have descended from Adam (Rom. 5:12). In a great theological leap he swept aside contemporary discriminations (Gal. 3:28; Eph. 2:12-17). Perhaps in nothing else do we see how radically Jesus changed Paul's attitudes.

The full quote for the poem Paul uses comes from a passage where Minos, the son of Zeus, honors his father. The author was the sixth-century B.C. Cretan poet Epimenides.

"They fashioned a tomb for thee, O Holy and high
    one—
The Cretans, always liars, evil beasts, idle bellies!
But thou art not dead; thou livest and abidest for ever,
For in thee we live and move and have our being."

The third-century B.C. poet Aratus created the second of Paul's quotes: "It is with Zeus that every one of us in every way has to do, for we are also his offspring." [5]

The apostle, perceiving in their philosophy ideas common to the one Creator-God of Christianity, disinfected them of their paganism, and baptized them in biblical concepts. He sought to meet the Athenians where they were and then to lead them to Jesus.

To the continuing encouragement of those who even today witness to the gospel, it worked. As he called his hearers away from idolatry (Acts 17:29) and declared the time of choice and judgment (verse 31), he pointed them to Jesus. And some believed (verse 34).

Paul's teaching that God has stayed near to all nations (verse 27) echoed his more elaborate treatment of the same theme in Romans 1:20-25. The conclusion that judgment will come in Jesus Christ also follows the reasoning of Romans 1:32.

Later Paul reflected on how difficult it was for both Gentile and Jew to accept Jesus and the cross event

(1 Cor. 1:21-26). On the hill of Mars they stumbled at the Resurrection. But not all. The wise waited to hear him further (verse 32).

Paul felt that the results might have been greater. His later convictions about simplicity and directness (1 Cor. 2:1-4) found their origin in the Athenian experience.

"At the close of his labors he looked for the results of his work. Out of the large assembly that had listened to his eloquent words, only three had been converted to the faith. He then decided that from that time he would maintain the simplicity of the gospel. He was convinced that the learning of the world was powerless to move the hearts of men, but that the gospel was the power of God to salvation." [6]

---

[1] *The SDA Bible Commentary,* Ellen G. White Comments, vol. 7, p. 918.

[2] Blaiklock, *Acts: An Introduction and Commentary,* p. 122.

[3] Marshall, *Acts: An Introduction and Commentary,* p. 268.

[4] Gaebelein, ed., *The Expositor's Bible Commentary,* vol. 9, p. 463.

[5] *Ibid.,* p. 476.

[6] *The SDA Bible Commentary,* Ellen G. White Comments, vol. 6, p. 1062.

The Word Prospers

Acts 18:1-19:41

Paul learned a great lesson in Athens. Remembering his small results there, he arrived in Corinth "in weakness and in much fear and trembling" (1 Cor. 2:3, RSV).

Now he had other questions to ponder. Did the gospel have the power he thought it had? Corinth, a hotbed of vice and debauchery, would test the power of the Spirit through Paul's ministry. As we start our study five points should be noted:

1. He faced the city's extreme worldliness and moral cynicism with only the gospel to support him (1 Cor. 2:2).

2. Corinth would prove whether the Lord could break through such barriers. Paul's most exalted literature flowed after Corinth.

3. The Stephanas family opened the gospel account, not just in Corinth, but in all Achaia (1 Cor. 16:15). The nearby port of Cenchrea had its own church (Rom. 16:1).

4. The majority of the converts were Gentiles. Many had not been processed through Judaism as God-fearers.

5. Paul notes among the followers of Christ few educated people (1 Cor. 1:26). The hungry poor and the overfed rich met at the Lord's Supper (1 Cor. 11:18-22).

Luke provides a historical anchor for his narrative. Claudius expelled the Jews in A.D. 49 (Acts 18:2). Suetonius, some 70 years later, said that the emperor banished them because of rioting at the instigation of one Chrestus. Most probably he failed to understand that the issue among the Jews was over Jesus Christ.

Corinth overlooked the isthmus connecting mainland Greece with Peloponnesus. Above the city rose a fortress of great strength. Wooden rollers permitted the dragging of small ships across the isthmus, thus shortening many voyages and avoiding fierce storms in the Mediterranean. Larger ships had their cargo unloaded and carried across.

The Romans captured Corinth in 196 B.C., and then leveled it in 146 B.C. when it revolted against the empire. In 46 B.C. Julius Caesar ordered it rebuilt. By the time of Paul, in less than 100 years, it had grown to 200,000 people. The city prospered greatly through its commerce. But immorality of every kind flourished. About 500 years before the coming of the gospel the Greeks adopted a new word for sexual immorality—to "Corinthianize."

The Gospel Wins Among Sinners
Acts 18:1-23

All rabbinical students had to learn a trade (Acts 18:2, 3). Rather than asking the way to the synagogue, Paul sought out other tentmakers (verse 3). The firm of Aquila and Priscilla traded in Rome, Corinth, and Ephesus, according to Acts and the Epistles.

Many references mention Priscilla (or the more formal Prisca, as Paul sometimes calls her) ahead of her husband. She therefore either had a social or wealth advantage over him, possessed the better business brain, or was the more effective lay evangelist.

Paul reasoned from the Scriptures each Sabbath (verse 4). We have a model for such an approach in Acts 13. After Silas and Timothy arrived (verse 5) to join him, the Jews opposed the evidence of Scripture, using God's name (verse 6). Paul then shook his garments toward them, stating that their act of blasphemy would bring judgment on them, but that he was cleared of responsibility (Eze. 18:20, 24).

The news from Thessalonica encouraged him

(1 Thess. 3:7-10), though he still had to deal with false expectations about the coming of Christ (1 Thess. 4:13-5:11) and slander against himself (1 Thess. 2:3-6). At this time Paul wrote his first letter to Thessalonica. In the second letter that followed a few weeks later, Paul stressed that the imminence of Christ's return should not cause confusion.

The move to the house of Titus Justus, right next door to the synagogue, would have provoked the Jews (Acts 18:7). Those who wanted to hear Paul would have to make a public decision in transferring from the synagogue. Each Sabbath it would have been interesting to watch the two congregations assembling. Did they meet at the same hour?

Though abuse mounted (verse 6), the Lord directed him to keep on with his work (verses 9, 10). The pattern of preaching, persecution, then escape or expulsion would not serve in this large city. So for a year and a half the Spirit held back the winds of strife while the gospel prospered.

"Gallio [verse 12] . . . had a pleasant character, but suffered from ill health. He died as a result of Nero's suspicions against the family. The date of his proconsulship can be fixed fairly accurately from an inscription found at Delphi, and it probably commenced in July, A.D. 51." [1]

The charge against Paul (verse 13) resurrected the claim that Christianity was not a legal religion. But the Roman emperor Claudius allowed the Jews to practice their religion outside of Rome, and Christianity was regarded as a Jewish sect. Therefore Gallio rejected the charge, citing the moral character of Paul and the Christians (verse 14). Like many Romans he looked at religious squabbles as beneath him (verse 15).

"If the apostle had at this time been compelled to leave Corinth, the converts to the faith of Jesus would have been placed in a perilous position. The Jews would have endeavored to follow up the advantage gained, even to the extermination of Christianity in that region." [2]

Finally in a peaceful parting, against the normal pattern, Paul set off for Syria and Antioch. At Cenchrea, the port for Corinth, Paul had his hair cut (verse 18). The Nazirite vow included abstinence from alcohol and a ban on the cutting of the hair.

"The chief impulse out of which vows have grown has often been a marked thankfulness for deliverance from danger following upon fear. The fear, the promise, and the deliverance have been noted in the record of Paul's work at Corinth, and a vow of consecration to the program of preaching the gospel would be a natural result. Paul neither despised nor condemned expressions of devout feeling, for he did not consider them legalistic, as he did certain other practices of the Jews." [3]

Facts and Fervor
Acts 18:24-19:22

The abilities of Apollos made him a considerable force in the early church. Even without the full facts, he proved a fervent and formidable advocate for Jesus. With more detail about the way of God (Acts 18:26) he witnessed with great conviction (verse 28).

In A.D. 41 Claudius had threatened Alexandrian Jews that he would proceed against them if they did not stop inviting Jews from Syria. Possibly the charge referred to Christian missionaries from Antioch beginning their mission in Alexandria. Apollos probably left Alexandria because of this decree.

In 1 Corinthians 2:1, 4, 5 Paul writes of the partisan spirit that developed in Corinth. Some of the congregation there exalted Apollos above Paul, showing both the man's ability and also the immaturity of the former pagans at Corinth.

The receiving of the Holy Spirit depended on a full knowledge of Jesus (Acts 19:2-5). The Spirit magnified the work of Apollos when he understood more fully (Acts

18:27, 28). So too with the dozen or so men who knew only John's baptism (Acts 19:6).

The Gospels carefully explain the right relationship between John the Baptist and Jesus (John 1:19-34; 3:22-36). The "one baptism" (Eph. 4:5) suggests that a sect existed that devoted itself to John, perhaps regarding him as an equal with Jesus. In the sixth and seventh centuries the Mandaeans claimed John as their prophet and founder.

The Spirit uses knowledge. The more we know, the better we present the appeal of the gospel, the more ably we answer questions. Because of his education and his training, Paul was a mighty tool in the hands of the Spirit.

"Then the apostle set before them the great truths that are the foundation of the Christian's hope. He told them of Christ's life on this earth and of His cruel death of shame. . . . He told them also of Christ's promise to send the Comforter, through whose power mighty signs and wonders would be wrought, and he described how gloriously this promise had been fulfilled on the day of Pentecost." [4]

Apollos and the followers of John the Baptist all showed a teachable spirit. For the third time tongues followed as Paul laid hands on the 12 men (Acts 19:6). As in the other two cases, John's disciples represented a new group receiving the Spirit. They spoke intelligible language—prophecy is always understandable.

Demonism and Diana—Paganism Challenged
Acts 19:7-21

In Ephesus Paul worked at the peak of his powers. There the devotees of Diana scrambled to preserve her influence against Christianity's advance. Indeed the whole province of Asia resounded with the evangelism of Paul. Magic, public or private, met its fate in the Christian witness. Pagan religion staggered at the blows of the Christian message. Paul challenged obdurate Judaism, demon possession, magic, entrenched paganism, each in its turn, and defeated them all.

Luke's missionary purposes are well served in this chapter. He invites consideration of the following:

1. Difficult situations may yield to the Spirit (Acts 19:9).

2. Effective urban ministries can influence large areas (verse 10).

3. The Spirit gives us company in our witness (verses 11, 12).

4. The name of Jesus is more powerful than any other (verses 13-19).

5. The will of God directs missionary effort (verse 21).

6. Entrenched anti-Christian systems yield to the gospel (verse 26).

7. Influential people of goodwill provide support for a worthy cause (verses 35-41).

Ephesus dated from the eleventh century B.C. Greek colonists from Athens founded it to open up trade with the interior of Asia Minor. Rome made it the provincial capital. In Paul's time the city's economic strength had already begun to slip as the harbor repeatedly silted up.

Besides trade, its other claim to fame was the magnificent temple to Diana (Greek—Artemis), one of the seven wonders of the ancient world. First built by Croesus, that legendary king of great wealth, about 550 B.C., by New Testament times it was four times larger than the Parthenon. As commerce declined the Ephesus temple dominated the prosperity of the city. Paul arrived in the city most likely during the summer of A.D. 54.

The apostle could not tolerate a dividing wall between Jew and Gentile (Eph. 2:14-16). He moved to neutral ground where both Jew and Gentile might hear the gospel. We may wonder whether even a Greek mother would name her child Tyrannus ("tyrant") (Acts 19:9). Perhaps Tyrannus was a local teacher or philosopher whose students nicknamed him thus.

Paul would probably have used the midday work break from about 11 a.m. to 4 p.m. to conduct his daily sessions. To them came inquirers. From them went the converted. Soon the whole province knew of Paul, the gospel, and the claims of Jesus Christ (verse 10).

The mind-set of the Ephesians had affected even Jews. The seven sons of Sceva tried "Jesus magic" on the demon-possessed, with dire results (verses 13-16). Paul had such influence in the city that they tried to enrich their attempted exorcism by linking his name to Jesus'.

"A Jewish chief priest would enjoy high prestige in magical circles, for he was the sort of person most likely to know the pronunciation of the Ineffable Name." [5]

A magical spell must have secrecy to exercise power. The deeper the secret, the more the power. By confessing that they had used magic spells, the converted broke their power (verse 18). Examples of such magical scrolls survive in collections in London, Paris, and Leiden. Usually they consist of meaningless arrangements of letters and numbers.

"How numerous are the books of infidel tendencies, which are calculated to unsettle the mind through specious doubts! . . . What a mass of fictitious reading is there in the world, to fill the mind with fancies and follies, thus creating a disrelish for the words of truth and righteousness!" "You have had your magical books, in which the very scenes and pictures were inspired by him who was once an exalted angel in the courts of heaven." [6]

A few bonfires of books, magazines, videotapes, and records might well be needed in many a Christian church!

For Paul, Rome was (verse 21) a stopping place on his way to the western end of the Mediterranean, where he hoped to evangelize Spain (Rom. 15:24, 28). The empire's capital already had Christian witnesses, and he avoided building on another man's foundation (Rom. 15:20).

The apostle planned to collect funds for the church in

Jerusalem (Acts 24:17; Rom. 15:25, 26; 1 Cor. 16:1, 2). Timothy and Erastus (Acts 19:22) prepared the way for his proposed journey to Macedonia (Phil. 2:24 may refer to the visit).

Riot and Reason
Acts 19:22-41

Acts has more than its share of selfish, money-oriented people who declare themselves devoted to God. Judas, Ananias and Sapphira, Elymas, and now Demetrius (Acts 19:24) carry on a theme begun by Luke in his Gospel. What Jesus censured in the Pharisees, the book of Acts condemns wherever found.

The assertion that the Christian movement was turning the world upside down occurred first in Thessalonica (Acts 17:6). Now Demetrius makes a similar charge (Acts 19:26). Luke chronicles the immense response to both the ministry of Jesus and the preaching of the gospel.

Nothing can stand in the way of God's plan. The picture of fierce opposition (verse 28) shows how powerful were the heavenly forces arrayed on the side of God's Man and His men. The words of Gamaliel expressed the theme in Acts: "If it is from God, you will never be able to put them down, and you risk finding yourselves at war with God" (Acts 5:39, NEB). Gamaliel was right.

Demetrius's fears (Acts 19:27) proved correct. Before long Diana lost her hold on Asia Minor. For centuries the Christian churches in the area staunchly defended the faith against pagan influences. It was to this area that Constantine went when he established an alternative capital to Rome. The strong Christian faith in the lands of the seven churches undid millennia of paganism.

Paul had helpers, Gaius of Derbe and Aristarchus of Thessalonica (Acts 20:4). They bore the brunt of the crowd's fury. But the crowd did not proceed to a lynching as on other occasions. Instead, they tried to form themselves into a meeting of the Ephesian people—the popular town assembly known from ancient Greek times (Acts 19:30).

The leaders did not know how to conduct business (verse 32). The Christians perceived this and prevented Paul from appearing at it (verse 30). The Asiarchs also advised against it (verse 31). These dignitaries arranged for athletic contests and ruled on appropriate acts of worshiping the emperor. Evidently, Paul had preached before them and influenced them favorably.

Confusion reigned (verse 32) and the people began to ask why they had come. Luke does not make clear just what role Alexander would have played (verse 33). Alexander may have been the coppersmith (2 Tim. 4:14) who did "much evil" against Paul. In that case, the Jews may have looked to him to make matters difficult for the apostle.

Luke appears to enjoy describing this episode. The inane shouting (verse 34), the discomfort of the Jews, and the general confusion delighted him as a story-teller, especially as no harm came either to Paul or the Christian movement.

In Ephesus the town clerk was the main magistrate of the city. He served as the liaison between its government and the Roman provincial administration also located in the city. The clerk's appearance immediately quieted the crowd (verse 35).

Facing the crowd's emotional outburst, the official used an argument similar to Gamaliel's (verses 36, 37). He also developed another theme of Luke's: the Christian church had done nothing treasonous (verse 39). Luke put such declarations of innocence in the mouths of prominent Roman officials.

The town clerk's speech may also have referred to a possible belief that Jews stole sacred objects from pagan shrines and temples (verse 37), and sold them for profit.

Gaius and Aristarchus, being Gentiles, (verse 29) could not be so accused.

In the modern world, where the occult and mysticism set their lures, Acts has profitable lessons. Simon Magus, Elymas, the sons of Sceva, and the magicians at Ephesus show that such practices had no part in early Christianity. Nor should they snare modern Christians.

"The mystic voices that spoke at Endor and at Ephesus are still by their lying words misleading the children of men. Could the veil be lifted from before our eyes, we should see evil angels employing all their arts to deceive and destroy. . . . The apostle's admonition to the Ephesian church should be heeded by the people of God today: 'Have no fellowship with the unfruitful works of darkness, but rather reprove them' (Eph. 5:11)." [7]

For Paul and the band of witnesses, Ephesus proved a great victory. News of what had happened went throughout the province. "In such ways the word of the Lord showed its power, spreading more and more widely and effectively" (Acts 19:20, NEB).

---

[1] Marshall, *Acts: An Introduction and Commentary*, p. 297.

[2] White, *The Acts of the Apostles*, p. 254.

[3] *The SDA Bible Commentary*, vol. 6, p. 365.

[4] White, *The Acts of the Apostles*, pp. 282, 283.

[5] Bruce, *The Book of the Acts*, p. 390.

[6] Ellen G. White, *Messages to Young People*, pp. 276, 277.

[7] ———, *The Acts of the Apostles*, p. 290.

For the Name of the Lord Jesus

Acts 20:1-21:25

In the lonely outreaches of Melanesia lies the grave of Norman Wiles. The Australian missionary with his American wife chose the fiercely pagan island of Malekula, now part of Vanuatu, as most in need of the gospel.

In a matter of months Norman was dead, and his wife, Alma, torn and bewildered, left the islands. Malaria had killed her beloved husband. What was left for her? How could she know the will of God?

Years later Alma Wiles returned to Malekula and visited the spot where a stone marker points out the sacrifice of her husband. Bands of singing Christians met her to assure her that even in that terrible loss God had found a way to fulfill His plans.

Those who observed Paul preparing to head for Jerusalem felt many misgivings. They tried to divert or stop him. Even the Holy Spirit seemed to be on their side.

The ill-fated trip began in disaster and finished with Paul in custody. Yet Paul soldiered on. Whatever came to him, he would endure for the name of the Lord Jesus.

Paul believed that the success of his mission among the Gentiles would make the Jews turn to Jesus from jealousy at what the Spirit was accomplishing outside of Israel (Rom. 11:14). In bringing a tribute of Gentile converts to Jerusalem he hoped to show how God was fulfilling prophecy.

"Now is there any explanation of these two circumstances—that Paul goes up personally with the gift at the serious risk of his life, and that on that journey he is accompanied by such a large group consisting of representatives of the Gentile churches? There is such an explanation, and it lies in Paul's view, expressed in Romans 11, of the connection between the mission to the Gentiles and the mission to the Jews. It is his intention to save the Jews by making them jealous of the Gentiles, who are accepting the gospel in great numbers; and now he is going up to the stronghold of Israel, to the disobedient [Rom. 11:30, RSV], as he calls them, with a representative company of believing Gentiles." [1]

The Constraint of the Spirit
Acts 20:1-27

Paul had a pastoral side of which Acts gives evidence. Chapter 20 explores the Paul who sought to maintain and strengthen the work already established.

With a band of Gentile representatives he set out for Jerusalem. He had the relief collection for Jerusalem with him, an added reason for plots against him (Acts 20:3). The large delegation called special meetings at Troas (verses 6, 7). An opportunity to meet and hear Paul drew the congregation together. Having already spent the feast of unleavened bread at Philippi (verse 6), he was making the most of what he knew would be his last visit to the region (verse 38).

The miracle of Eutychus reminds us of similar ones performed by Elijah and Elisha (1 Kings 17:21; 2 Kings 4:34, 35). Paul threw himself on the young man and put his arms around him (Acts 20:10). Once the young man was restored, the meeting went on.

Those who insist that either verses 7 or 11 refer to the Lord's Supper are reading more into the record than the language requires. The meal may just as well have been the so-called love feast, famous among Christians of that age, at which slaves and the very poor feasted at the generosity of wealthier members of the congregation. Or it may have been the ordinary evening meal, delayed by the eagerness to hear as much from Paul as possible.

Though the early church had an organized life, we have to avoid reading modern church structures back into the record. The "elders" (verse 17) paralleled the elders of the synagogue. The "overseers" (verse 28) referred to the same people, relating to function rather than office. The elders oversaw, or guarded, the flock of God.

The farewell words divide into two parts. Verses 17 to 24 glance back at the life of the great missionary, while verses 25 to 35 look ahead to the future of the church.

Paul offered himself as an example to the elders (verses 18, 19), something he did more than once (1 Cor. 11:1; Phil. 4:9). Important character traits that he felt all should develop included:

1. Service for the Lord with humility (Acts 20:19). He did not deflect suffering onto others, but bore it himself (verse 19), just as the Lord had done.

Paul called himself the servant of the Lord (Rom. 1:1). Elsewhere, he mentioned that he served in humility (1 Thess. 2:6) and with tears (Phil. 3:18). Luke, knowing Paul well, caught not just the essentials of this farewell discourse but the very thoughts of the great man.

2. A desire that each congregation understand fully the message of salvation (Acts 20:20). Paul could present unpopular truths and argue them persuasively (Gal. 4:16; Acts 11:4).

Paul used the word *repentance* (Acts 20:21) to cover *conversion* (1 Thess. 1:9). *Faith* dominates Romans and is first in his great trilogy of Christian virtues, *faith, hope,* and *love.*

3. Submission to the Spirit, which should rule the life of the leader. He knew, both from external testimony (Acts 20:23) and direct from the Spirit (verse 22), that the guidance of the Spirit could put one's life at risk (verse 24).

4. Recognition that some values exceed even the worth of one's own life (verse 24). The apostle did not know whether the sufferings awaiting him would lead to death (verses 22, 24; 2 Tim. 4:7).

Fears for the Future
Acts 20:28-38

Paul had warned the Ephesians (Acts 20:26), had kept back nothing (verse 27), and had revealed all of God's purpose to them (verse 27; Eph. 1:11). Thus he¹ could declare himself free from the blood of all men (Acts 20:26; Eze. 33:1-6).

He had already told them what to expect in the future and how to act when things happened in accord with what he had revealed.

1. Leaders should remember the price paid for the congregation that they shepherd (Acts 20:28, 29). The church is "the church of God" (1 Cor. 1:2), and the cost was the blood of God's own Son (Rom. 8:32).

2. False teachings would invade the church and develop within it (Acts 20:30, 31). Later Timothy had to deal with that very problem at Ephesus (1 Tim. 1:3; 2 Tim. 2:15), one that persisted into the next generation (Rev. 2:1-7).

3. The future lay secure in God's hands (Acts 20:32), but would leaders fully trust Him? The gospel of grace (verses 24, 32) will build the Christian into full maturity (Eph. 4:12). It also will give an inheritance (Acts 20:32; Rom. 8:17). Moses' sermon linked the holy ones of God with the inheritance of Jacob (Deut. 33:3, 4).

4. Paul would participate in the promised inheritance (Acts 20:32), but did not ask to share other people's goods now (verse 33; 1 Cor. 9:15-18). Like Peter he did not possess silver or gold (Acts 3:6). He might have rightly claimed support from the congregations, but preferred to earn his own keep (Acts 20:34). The kindness of others he valued, but it left him embarrassed (Phil. 4:10-20), because

God had always provided.

5. It is better to give than to amass wealth beyond one's immediate needs (Acts 20:35). Paul quoted Jesus to point down the path of right Christian behavior in the marriage relationship, Christian stewardship, and honorable business dealings (1 Cor. 7:10; 9:14; 1 Tim. 5:18).

The farewell is touching in its intimacy and detail (Acts 20:36-38). Only those who have watched loved ones fly off to distant lands can understand the intensity of emotion portrayed here.

"Paul carried with him the atmosphere of heaven. All who associated with him felt the influence of his union with Christ. The fact that his own life exemplified the truth he proclaimed gave convincing power to his preaching. Here lies the power of truth. The unstudied, unconscious influence of a holy life is the most convincing sermon that can be given in favor of Christianity. Argument, even when unanswerable, may provoke only opposition; but a godly example has a power that it is impossible wholly to resist." [2]

Welcome and Praise
Acts 21:1-25

Paul journeyed to Jerusalem "under the constraint of the Spirit" (Acts 20:22, NEB). Jesus had gone into the wilderness to face temptation "led by the Spirit" (Luke 4:1). The apostle went to Jerusalem aware that it would be a time of trial and temptation for him.

He spoke of his journey to Jerusalem in Romans 15:25. His priestly service called for him to offer the Gentiles as "an acceptable sacrifice, consecrated by the Holy Spirit" (verse 16, NEB). The converts he had made displayed the results of that priestly work to all.

But the Spirit did not communicate only with Paul. He had already revealed the situation to the churches. Having understood through the Spirit what would happen to Paul, the disciples urged the apostle to cancel his trip to Jerusalem (Acts 21:4).

"This is where we have to ask the reasons for Paul's resolve to go in person. The purpose of the collection and its ultimate fortune were intimately connected with a question already hotly debated at the apostolic assembly—was the gospel without the Law proclaimed by Paul among the Gentiles a true gospel? . . . Were Gentiles, too, members of full and unconditional standing in the body of Christ? . . . His resolve shows the extent to which the unity of the church had continued as the unwavering objective of his endeavors." [3]

Paul linked the monetary contribution to meet the needs of God's people (2 Cor. 9:12) with the honor brought by obedience to the gospel (verse 13). He contemplated the unifying effect of the tribute of money and souls (verse 14).

"We are struck, too, by the noble perspectives of his vision: he already sees as a reality the benefaction of the Corinthian church, the thanksgivings of the Jerusalem Christians, their glorifying of God, and their response of prayer and affection for their Gentile brothers in Christ." [4]

We can imagine the prayer season on the beach at Tyre (Acts 21:5). So much to pray about, so many to pray for. The example of prayer by Jesus and the apostles indicates that nothing must happen without being prefaced by prayers. Through prayer the Spirit may act more effectively between us and the future, between us and the world, between us and the church.

Paul listed the gifts of the Spirit in 1 Corinthians 12. Acts shows almost all of them in action:

1. "The word of wisdom": Paul refrained from getting involved in the commotion over Diana (Acts 19:30).

2. "The word of knowledge": the instruction given Apollos (Acts 18:26).

3. "Faith": the conversion of the Philippian jailer (Acts 16:30, 31).

4. "The gifts of healing": the healings at Ephesus (Acts

19:11, 12).

5. "Prophecy": Philip's four prophetess daughters and Agabus (Acts 21:8-12).

6. "The working of miracles": the deliverance from the viper bite on Malta (Acts 28:3-6).

7. "The discerning of spirits": the exorcism of the slave girl at Philippi (Acts 16:18).

Agabus acted out his prophecy as was the manner of some of the Old Testament prophets (Isa. 20; Jer. 13:1-11). Our Lord predicted the fate and manner of the death of Peter (John 21:18, 19). And now, under the power of the Holy Spirit, Agabus predicted Paul's fate. Soon the Jews would try to lynch him, and he would escape only because he would be rescued by Roman soldiers. But in the end the Gentiles held Paul prisoner and would eventually execute him.

At the crisis hour in Gethsemane, when all had seemed against Him, Jesus had prayed, "Your will, not Mine, be done." Now, at the final moment of decision in Caesarea, Paul made the same choice and submitted himself to the will of God (Acts 21:13, 14). Those who had previously urged him to turn back now accepted his decision, and prayed the prayer of Gethsemane: "The will of the Lord be done" (verse 14). Paul's trip to Jerusalem paralleled Jesus' own fated last journey.

The apostle received a good welcome in Jerusalem (verse 17). Luke does not comment about how the Jerusalem leadership received the collection, though the Gentiles with Paul obviously created a problem. Jerusalem did not regard the relief money and the delegation in the way that he had expected.

"And he could not count upon the sympathy and support of even his own brethren in the faith." "It was apparent to Paul and his companions that even among those before whom they now stood were some who were unable to appreciate the spirit of brotherly love that had prompted the gifts." [5]

The Galatian Epistle may have reached Jerusalem by this time. The elders had reached the conclusion that Jews and even Jewish Christians could misinterpret both the theology and activities of Paul (verse 21). In response to his successes among the Gentiles (verse 19), the leaders pointed to their own (verse 20). Should Paul's visit put such great gains at risk? The scattering of Acts 8 had been reversed. Now thousands of converts lived in Jerusalem.

Paul had declared the end of the law as a system of righteousness (Rom. 10:4), but nowhere did he dissuade Jewish Christians from circumcising their children or following other national customs. He urged toleration (Rom. 14:7-12). The accusation being circulated in Jerusalem (Acts 21:21) had no substance.

Several suggestions have been made about what Paul actually did when he involved himself with the vow of the four men. The most satisfactory places the men at the conclusion of a Nazirite vow, which normally ran for 30 days. One scholar offers a reasonable sequence of events.

"The expense, which they could not afford, was to be assumed by Paul (the assumption of such expense counted as a pious deed); he had only to report this to the priest concerned and agree upon the time of absolution. Since Paul had come from abroad, he was, however, considered as levitically unclean. He had therefore first to regain levitical purity by a purification ritual. . . . Only when he was levitically clean could Paul be present at the absolution ceremony for the four." [6]

Unfortunately the clever plan (verses 23, 24) would go awry. "The Spirit of God did not prompt this instruction; it was the fruit of cowardice." [7]

The Spirit constrains, and God leads on. But what if men seek their own solutions and do not search for any divine blueprint? The question hangs over all human decisions, whether personal, family, or church. We risk far too much when we try our own wisdom. But we gain so much when we trust to divine wisdom. The gifts of the

Spirit that had accompanied Paul through his mission were available to guide the leaders of the church in Jerusalem. If we do not accept the gifts, what fearful consequences may descend on us, our loved ones, or the church we love?

---

[1] Johannes Munck, *Paul and the Salvation of Mankind,* p. 303.

[2] White, *The Acts of the Apostles,* pp. 510, 511.

[3] Gunther Bornkamm, *Paul,* pp. 92, 93.

[4] Philip E. Hughes, *Paul's Second Epistle to the Corinthians,* p. 341.

[5] White, *The Acts of the Apostles,* pp. 398-400.

[6] Haenchen, *The Acts of the Apostles,* p. 612.

[7] White, *The Acts of the Apostles,* p. 404.

Turmoil and Trial

Acts 21:26-23:35

When people who ought to know encourage you to do something and it all goes wrong, it is easy to portion out blame. The apostle might have done that. James and the other Jewish Christians had urged him on a dangerous course. As Paul had the voice of the Spirit cautioning him all the way to Jerusalem, so he might have expected that his brothers in the capital also received their directions from the Spirit.

Not so. And Paul became the victim of others' poor judgment. Yet God always has plans for His children, even though they make mistakes, or others make them on their behalf.

We hear no more of James and his associates. Like Peter earlier, he simply steps out of the picture. We do not know if the Jewish Christians remembered Peter's imprisonment and prayed for Paul. The great hero was isolated and new forces surrounded him. No Barnabas or Silas shared his cell. No Timothy or John Mark assisted him. Paul, alone with the Spirit, and with his faith fixed on Jesus, now met the greatest test of his stormy career.

When Things Go Wrong
Acts 21:26-40

The business of the vow (Acts 21:26) took him through the city frequently. Jews from the province of Asia, also there for the feast, had spotted him with Trophimus, one of their countrymen. When they later saw him in the

Temple, they assumed that Trophimus must be around somewhere too (verse 29).

In Madurai, India, at the Temple of a Thousand Pillars, a curtain hides an inner sanctuary. Only Hindus may enter. Westerners attempting to enter would create a riot just as easily as did the charge laid against Paul (verse 30).

Herod had constructed an open space where Gentiles might come and admire the Temple. Beyond this Court of the Gentiles lay the Court of the Women. Between the two a barrier read, "No man of alien race is to enter within the balustrade and fence that goes round the Temple, and if anyone is taken in the act, let him know that he has himself to blame for the penalty of death that follows."

The Romans accepted the warning and allowed the Jews to enforce the threat. Paul knew this very well and would not have risked Trophimus' life by such a rash deed.

The threefold charge—this fellow has attacked the people, the law, and the sanctuary—has an ancient ring to it (verse 28). It would be the work of the great apostate (Dan. 7:25; 8:11-14). Paul, who would soon proclaim the Messiah (Acts 22:14), was slandered with the accusation that he was doing the deeds of the abomination, the apocalyptic opposer of the Messiah.

"The Levite Temple guard was arranged in three groups: (a) doorkeepers at the outer door of the Temple; (b) guards at the 'rampart'; (c) patrols in the Court of Gentiles, and no doubt by day in the Court of Women also. . . . The men who dragged Paul out of 'sanctuary' *(i.e.,* the Court of Women) and closed the gates leading to the Court of Gentiles (Acts 21:30), during the riot leading to his arrest, were obviously members of the Temple police, more precisely the posts mounted at the 'rampart' during daytime." [1]

The fortress of Antonia stood to the northwest of the Temple. In Paul's day it housed a cohort of Roman soldiers (about 600 men). Two flights of steps led from the fortress to the Court of Gentiles. In a matter of minutes the guard could be (and was in the case of Paul) on the scene and in control of any sudden uproar (Acts 21:31-33).

Soldiers carried off the sore and bruised Paul (verse 33), their bodies protecting him from the brickbats and broken pieces of pottery that always seemed on hand when a lynching was in the air. The detachment sent to rescue Paul numbered at least 200 men because it contained more than one centurion (verse 32).

The Egyptian (verse 38) was possibly the false prophet called Ben Stada in the Talmud. He claimed that the multitude would bring down the walls of the city like Jericho's in Joshua's day. Josephus speaks of a force of 30,000 led against Jerusalem. Felix dispersed the mob at a cost of about 400 deaths. Luke's more modest figure of 4,000 may be more accurate. In Greek the signs for 4,000 and 30,000 can be easily confused.[2]

In the years before the fall of Jerusalem organized bands of *knife men* ("murderers," verse 38) mingled with the crowds in Jerusalem. Especially at the feasts they would stab pro-Roman Jews, their chief enemies.

Paul had never flinched from confronting mobs. In Ephesus the believers had to restrain him from venturing out in one (Acts 19:30). His fluent and cultured Greek convinced the commandant that he was no vicious thug (Acts 21:37). Now his equally fluent and polished Hebrew created respect and quiet as he spoke (Acts 22:1, 2). Never had Paul put his erudition to such good use. The very power of God flowed through him, and his listeners sensed it.

Witness and Experience
Acts 22:1-30

Paul made two points:

1. No one could doubt that he was truly a Hebrew of the Hebrews (Acts 22:2). He was a Jew, would not forget it, and was proud of it (2 Cor. 11:22; Phil. 3:4, 5).

Gamaliel (Acts 22:3) had died about A.D. 58. A grandson of the great rabbi Hillel, his fame as a scholar continues to this day. He was the first rabbi given the title Rabban, "our great one," rather than rabbi, "my master."

Paul earlier had operated under the personal authority of the high priest and the council of elders (verse 5). Christians of that time considered themselves Jews, and were thought of as a troublesome but nonetheless Jewish sect. Saul, the future apostle, needed letters of authority to arrest and arraign Christian Jews (verses 4, 5).

2. But Paul had changed. The difference came from his encounter with Jesus of Nazareth (verse 8). Because Jesus conversed with him, He had clearly risen from death and was thus speaking from heaven. Therefore Paul had been attacking not only Jesus but God (verses 6, 7).

Only this account records Paul's question "What shall I do?" (verse 10). Paul wanted his audience to know that he acted under the guidance of Jesus as a heavenly being (verse 10).

Ananias, a Jew of impeccable qualifications (verses 12, 13) had sheltered and instructed him. Paul was accumulating evidence that divine forces had led him from the time of his vision.

The apostle to the Gentiles said nothing of the Christian accusation that the rulers of the Jews had murdered the Messiah. The crowd, therefore, listened attentively, and perhaps even with respect—Paul had experienced something that none of them had (verse 14).

Even the commission to witness to all men (verse 15), both to Jews and Gentiles, did not upset the crowd. It was an age of Jewish proselytizing, and the language could refer to a normal Jewish mission.

Stephen (verse 20) had declared the Temple not just irrelevant but also a snare because it had become an object of worship. Now Paul declared Jesus as Lord of the Temple (verses 17, 18). The hearing Jews should look to the Lord of the Temple rather than the Temple itself.

Paul's argument had introduced a new justification for the Christian mission. In the very Temple itself he had heard the command to go to the Gentiles (verse 21). Thus he established a progression from Judaism to Christianity that showed they were part of the one divine process.

But in the end his declaration of the command of Jesus that authorized his mission to the Gentiles only outraged the Jews. It was one thing to exalt Judaism and attract Gentiles into the God-fearing relationship so common in that age but quite another to establish a direct relationship of God to Gentiles.

The Jews concluded that the original accusation about bringing Trophimus into the Temple might be true, despite Paul's denials. If Jesus was Lord of the Temple and had authorized an independent mission to the Gentiles, then Paul would see nothing wrong with bringing them to the Temple to worship its Lord. "Kill him!" they yelled (verse 22), just as a previous crowd had shouted "Crucify Him!"

One can only stand in amazement at the wisdom of God in choosing and anointing Paul. Protected first by being able to speak Greek, then getting a hearing by speaking Hebrew, gaining honor by his association with Gamaliel, the apostle now prevented further injury and commanded respect from the imperial forces by revealing his Roman citizenship (verses 25-29).

Government and Innocence
Acts 23:1-35

Readers of Acts find themselves saying, "Can't they see that this man is innocent? Isn't it obvious?"

Luke had that aim in mind when he wrote of the trial of Jesus. He approached Paul's various appearances in the same way. In no way could Paul be guilty. Prejudice and pressure prevented him from receiving fair treatment.

During his ministry Jewish and Gentile mobs had

attacked him a number of times. Stones had beaten him to the ground; his back had bled from the whips of legal authorities. Now, no sooner had he begun his speech than servants of the high priest began to beat him (Acts 23:2).

Paul declared his conscience quite clear (verse 1). In the Epistles Paul also considered his conscience and how it had judged him (2 Cor. 1:12; 4:2; Rom. 2:15).

Josephus views Ananias, the high priest, in a negative light. He used questionable approaches to get the people on his side. Insolent and quick-tempered, his reaction here (Acts 23:2) fits the man perfectly. Paul's claim of innocence might have offended Ananias, or it might have irked him to be addressed as just one of the brothers.

While we may express surprise at Paul's seemingly hot answer, we have no right to expect sinless perfection from him. However, we may be reading the incident wrongly if we look on it as an outburst of temper or an overly hostile answer hardly in keeping with his own standard: "They curse us, and we bless; they persecute us, and we submit to it; they slander us, and we humbly make our appeal. We are treated as the scum of the earth, the dregs of humanity, to this very day" (1 Cor. 4:12, 13, NEB).

Paul as prophet may have seen the fate of Ananias—he died an unpleasant death a few years later. He may have spoken in irony—a man who would give an order for an innocent person to be struck could not be a high priest. Surely he would have known both the dress and the person of the high priest (verse 4).

Jesus had referred to Pharisees as whitewashed tombs (Matt. 23:27). In Ezekiel God compares Israel to a wall daubed with untempered mortar (Eze. 13:10-16). Ananias was a Sadducee and particularly unbending toward the minor faults of others.

Paul raised the question of the resurrection, placing himself squarely with the Pharisaic faction (verses 6-8). Instantly the Pharisees came out on the side of Paul's theology. Not quite believing that Jesus had appeared to him, they conceded that an angel or spirit might have spoken to him (verse 9). Chaos ruled as Pharisee and Sadducee battled it out in words. The Romans hustled Paul off to prison again (verse 10).

Luke records a number of visions that Paul had: the vision on the road to Damascus, the vision in the Temple, the vision of the man from Macedonia, the vision at Corinth, and a shipboard vision. Now he experienced one in prison (verse 11). Each one came at a critical moment in his life, more than once when danger threatened.

Paul appeared in Jerusalem as a witness to Jesus (verse 11). His tormentors might call it a trial, and we might look upon it as a travesty of justice, but the Lord saw it as confessing His name. In the courts of glory He acknowledges the faithful witness (Luke 12:8, 9). The word *witness* fills an important role in Luke's understanding of the response of the Christian to the gospel of the grace of God.

"The apostle could never forget his conversion from a persecutor of all who believe in Christ, to a believer in Him. What a bearing this conversion had on all his afterlife! What an encouragement it was as he worked on the side of Him whom he once ridiculed and despised. . . . He could speak intelligently because he had an experience, a personal knowledge, of the Lord Jesus Christ." [3]

The providences of God now show how the Lord was preserving the apostle for that witness in Rome. A conspiracy sought to take advantage of a further hearing before the council (Acts 23:13-15). It would have been fairly easy to dispatch Paul if determined men got near him. A dagger in the crowd, a sudden dash past the Roman bodyguard, a missile from a balcony—the opportunities were there, hence the danger.

The tiny window that now opens on Paul's family tells us that his relatives were highly placed (verse 16). The lad had access to extremists in the council determined to get rid of Paul. The boy's connections let him visit Paul in the prison, and following that, the commandant himself (verses 16, 17).

Lysias (verse 26) knew Ananias. Thinking it altogether likely that such an attempt would be made, he clamped down on security (verse 22). The seriousness of his response to the threat shows what kind of man the high priest was and also the force that fanatic Jews might be expected to mount. Two hundred regular infantry, 70 cavalry, and an additional 200 light infantry could deal with any foreseeable assault (verses 23, 24).

He acted immediately. Under cover of darkness, that very night (verse 31), the escort left. The frustrated conspirators had no idea of the escape until the following morning.

The cavalcade made good time during the night, covering about 35 miles to the village of Antipatris at the foot of the Judean hills (verse 31).

Only after Felix had ascertained that Paul came from Cilicia (verse 34) did he take on the case. Had Paul come from Syria or one of the kingdoms in Asia Minor rather than from Tarsus, Felix would have had to send Paul on to them. Paul's Roman citizenship now played a large part in taking him on his way to Rome.

The list of unsavory characters in Acts grows longer as we add the name of Felix. Tacitus, the Roman historian, says that he practiced every kind of cruelty and lust. "He wielded the power of a king with the instincts of a slave." His second wife was Drusilla, the youngest daughter of Herod Agrippa I.

Luke observed all this, probably hastening on to Caesarea as soon as he knew what had happened. His eyewitness accounts make this portion of Acts dramatic.

Though God was continuing to work on behalf of Paul, seeking to maximize his contribution, events had now limited what might otherwise have been even more fruitful.

"Had the leaders in the church fully surrendered their feeling of bitterness toward the apostle, and accepted him as one specially called of God to bear the gospel to the Gentiles, the Lord would have spared him to them. . . . How often would the Lord have prolonged the work of some faithful minister, had his labors been appreciated! But if the church permits the enemy of souls to pervert the understanding, so that they misrepresent and misinterpret the words and acts of the servant of Christ; if they allow themselves to stand in his way and hinder his usefulness, the Lord sometimes removes from them the blessing which He gave." [4]

---

[1] Joachim Jeremias, *Jerusalem in the Time of Jesus*, pp. 209, 210.

[2] F. F. Bruce, *The Acts of the Apostles*, p. 398.

[3] *The SDA Bible Commentary*, Ellen G. White Comments, vol. 6, p. 1065.

[4] White, *The Acts of the Apostles*, pp. 417, 418.

For Jesus' Sake

Acts 24:1-25:27

The Spirit works within the world to convince of sin, of righteousness, and of coming judgment. He is effective. We know that. Great systems of morality, like Buddhism and Confucianism, do not offer salvation. However, they represent the protection of the Spirit against the total decadence and debauchery of mankind.

Where the grace of God flows, there the Spirit strives with individuals. As grace has appeared to all men in the person of Jesus Christ, so the Spirit seeks all, to bring them that grace in a form that will convict and convert.

The last time Luke mentioned the Spirit in the epic of Paul was when He spoke through Agabus about future threats to the apostle's safety (Acts 21:11). He has not withdrawn from the field, however.

We have found Him in Paul's unexpected freedom to address the crowd at the Temple (Acts 22:1). He opened Paul's mind to a vision of the Lord Jesus the following night (Acts 23:11). The Spirit turns annoyance into sympathy (verse 29). And He gives courage to a youth (verse 16). It remains Luke's intention to show that, despite human bunglings and connivings, God has directed all to His glory through the Spirit.

Hope for All
Acts 24:1-27

The butter-smooth Tertullus constructed a straw man he called Paul. But his fabrication failed to depict either the true events or the true apostle.

Tertullus's flattery could hardly have been less appropriate because (1) if Judea enjoyed "great quiet-ness" (Acts 24:2), Felix had achieved it by stifling even legitimate protests; (2) the "worthy deeds" included ruthless murder and unspeakable vice (verse 2); and (3) the "thankfulness" (verse 3) came from those who escaped his cruelty.

Ananias's spokesman brought three charges against Paul: (1) he was a complete nuisance (verse 5), a pest, responsible for riots and uprisings all over the empire; (2) he was a ringleader of the Nazarene sect (verse 5), presumably known to Felix; and (3) he had profaned the Temple, a crime acknowledged as most serious by the Romans (verse 6).

Jesus was called the Nazarene because He came from Nazareth. Tertullus was making the point that while Judaism had Roman approval, the breakaway, heretical Christian sect did not.

The charge of profaning the Temple had created the riot that led to Paul's arrest. It had no substance, but Tertullus did not find it difficult to find perjurers (verse 9).

Also Tertullus brought a charge against Lysias. The Roman official had interfered with the Jews' right to deal with those who profaned the holy places of the Temple (verse 7). Furthermore, he had done so with violence, giving orders that the Jews must refer to Felix something over which they had jurisdiction. Lysias and Paul were available for cross-examination as were the witnesses.

Felix did have experience with Jewish matters. He had ruled the province for about 10 years at this point. Whether Paul knew his true character we cannot know. He could do little but hope that Felix' understanding of the situation would lead to his release.

Paul began his defense by stating that he had arrived in Jerusalem only 12 days earlier (verse 11). He had come neither for sedition nor rebellion, but for worship. Not only was he not guilty of attacking the holy people, but he had come to give alms on their behalf (verse 17). Paul had used the Temple for worship as a devout Jew might (verse 18), and had supported everything written in the Law and the Prophets (verse 14). Thus he directed part of his defense past Felix to Ananias and his entourage.

Rather than acting in accord with the abomination of desolation foretold by Daniel the prophet, he was seeking the best good of Israel, the holy place, and the law (verses 12-15).

The apostle denied that the way they called heresy (verse 14) perverted the teachings of the Jewish Scripture. Jesus' own explanations (Luke 24:27, 44) featured an extensive use of the Psalms and the words of the prophets as did the sermons following Pentecost.

Behind the charade mounted by Ananias, Paul discerned a deeper issue. The Jewish leaders who accepted the doctrine of the resurrection had fallen into a trap. The evidence of Jesus' resurrection, with multiple witnesses and other proofs, pressed in on them. If Jesus had risen, how could they then deny that He was Messiah (Acts 24:21)?

At the beginning Peter and the other apostles had come close to moving the whole populace to accept Jesus as Messiah (Acts 5:12-16). The church had not yet abandoned the hope that at least the majority of Jews would see the light (Acts 21:20). Most of the people accepted the resurrection of the dead (Acts 24:21).

Paul defended his veracity in the light of the judgment. Inherent in his words was the prospect of review or investigation (verses 15, 16). He strived to keep his conscience clear because up ahead the scanning, discerning eye of God would review his works.

Few ever possess Paul's sense of moral uprightness (verse 16). However, even that will to do right could fail him (Rom. 7:15-23).

The story contrasts the good conscience of Paul with

the smitten one of Felix (Acts 24:16, 25). The Spirit works to guide a life committed to Christ in righteousness, while He troubles the one that demands its own way. As Paul presented faith in Christ (verses 24, 25) and reasoned about eternal issues, Felix trembled.

"With terrible distinctness there came up before him the secrets of his early life of profligacy and bloodshed, and the black record of his later years. He saw himself licentious, cruel, rapacious. Never before had the truth been thus brought home to his heart. . . . But instead of permitting his convictions to lead him to repentance, he sought to dismiss these unwelcome reflections." [1]

A sordid story also is told about Drusilla, Felix's wife. She had married King Azizus of Emesa while still quite young. Felix met her and, captivated by her beauty, hired a magician, Atomus, to seduce her away from her husband. The plan succeeded, and while still a teenager she became the second wife of Felix. She was the sister of Herod Agrippa II and Bernice (Acts 25:13).

While the humble Philippian jailer found salvation as he quivered with fear, Felix waited for the fear to lessen and then dismissed the chance of eternal life. The Holy Spirit can only bring us to a sense of our need; He cannot make the decision in favor of eternal life on our behalf.

Although Paul remained under house arrest (Acts 24:23), he had considerable liberty much as the authorities later granted him at Rome (Acts 28:30, 31). The house arrest lasted two years (Acts 24:27).

Persuasion or Procrastination
Acts 25:1-27

Festus far surpassed in character both Felix and those who succeeded Festus. Lucceius Albinus followed him, and history records his villainy. Gessus Florus, the next in line, milked Palestine of its wealth through corruption and bribery. However, Festus reigned with an even hand, and most regretted his untimely death in A.D. 62. In some measure the succession of inept, greedy, and vicious rulers resulted in the sacking of Jerusalem in A.D. 70. Given wiser rulers, that tragedy might not have occurred.

The Roman governor saw through the plot to have Paul brought to Jerusalem (Acts 25:3). He required any who wished to charge Paul to go with him to Caesarea (verse 5).

The smoldering resentment against the Christian movement surfaced in the continued attempts to have Paul condemned. Jesus had created a devoted band of witnesses who would neither give up their faith nor go away. The charges leveled against the apostle applied to Christians as a whole.

Wherever Christianity and traditional Judaism competed, charges one, two, and three rolled out: Christians attack the Law, Christians profane the Temple, and Christians are seditious (verse 8). Wherever he protests the charges or his judges declare him innocent, read *the church* for Paul. The church strenuously denied that it wanted the Law of Moses removed from Jewish practice, the Temple physically destroyed, and that the members had any plans to rebel.

Festus, perhaps ignorant of the danger it would bring to Paul, proposed that the apostle should go to Jerusalem for judgment before the Sanhedrin.

Paul did not wish to escape the just penalty of the law (verse 10). (In fact, he would face death if that should be the judgment.) What he did not want was rough, frontier-type justice, where governors toadied to corrupt high priests and mob rule held sway.

"A Roman citizen anywhere in the empire was protected against summary magisterial punishment *(Coercitio)*, although the provincial magistrate might deal with cases which involved a plain breach of established statute law (which Paul's case manifestly did not). . . . The picture given in Acts is true to the dramatic date of the book; the case of Paul's appeal fits in with what we know of conditions in the late fifties of the first Christian century, and Luke's account of it is . . . a substantial contribution to the available evidence." [2]

New to the situation, Festus knew nothing of the plottings and lies that had put the apostle in prison. Therefore the appeal to Caesar (verse 11) caught him by surprise. However, his council knew the Roman law about its citizens (verse 12). Once the appeal was lodged, he had to concur. To Rome Paul would go.

"In the future, men claiming to be Christ's representatives will take a course similar to that followed by the priests and rulers in their treatment of Christ and the apostles. . . . All who in that evil day will fearlessly serve God according to the dictates of conscience will need courage, firmness, and a knowledge of God and His Word; for those who are true to God will be persecuted, their motives will be impugned, their best efforts misinterpreted, and their names cast out as evil." [3]

Paul, by his own activities, had helped sharpen the line between Christianity and Judaism. A favorable hearing in Rome might give legitimacy to the church in its own right. And if Caesar himself heard Paul's case, what might not happen?

Now the Herods again entered Christian history (verse 13). Herod Agrippa II ruled one of the petty kingdoms in the area, but he had in his power the right to appoint the high priests and to keep charge of the ceremonial robes used on the annual Day of Atonement. As a Jew he had schooled himself on Jewish law and religion.

Luke included Festus's comments to Agrippa (verses 16-21) for a reason. The speech informed his readers of their legal position and also spoke kindly of the Roman system of justice. We are not yet in the time of the Revelation, where Roman tyrants had already taken the lives of believers.

The arguments between Paul and his accusers had left Festus confused (verse 19). He discerned the main point under contention, but failed completely to catch its significance (verse 20). The claim of resurrection obviously did not register with him.

The Roman official hoped that Agrippa, an acknowledged expert on Jewish matters, might help him (verse 26). As yet he had not even been able to formulate any sensible charge that Caesar or his advisers might understand. What was there in Roman law that would relate to the case (verse 27)?

Reading of Paul's appearance before Agrippa II reminds us of Jesus' before Herod Antipas (Luke 23:6-14). Each stood before a Roman governor and each was brought to a Jewish king who greatly wanted to meet the accused. It would be typical of Luke to find and use this parallel. However, the stories depart from each other after the initial similarities. In no way does Agrippa's rather kind handling of Paul compare with the curt and cynical way Antipas treated our Lord.

A splendid opportunity for the gospel now opened. Anyone of importance in Caesarea attended the court that day (verse 23). The occasion was ceremonial. Finery bedecked the governor's palace. Agrippa and Bernice in their royal purple and the golden crowns of their royal status and Festus in his scarlet robes held center stage. City leaders, the Jews of Agrippa's entourage, officers of the five Roman cohorts stationed in Caesarea—all stood arrayed in their finest.

Now into this pomp and circumstance they bring the little rabbi, Paul, his hands in chains, his features marked and weathered with the passing of the years and the hardships he had endured. But he holds the attention of all as the Spirit fills him. When Christ rules the heart and the Spirit fills the life, the Christian has a power and a presence none can match.

"In this man, apparently without friends or wealth or position, and held a prisoner for his faith in the Son of God, all heaven was interested. Angels were his attendants. Had the glory of one of those shining messengers flashed forth, the pomp and pride of royalty would have paled; king and courtiers would have been stricken to the earth, as were the Roman guards at the sepulcher of Christ." [4]

---

[1] White, *The Acts of the Apostles*, pp. 425, 426.

[2] F. F. Bruce, *Paul, Apostle of the Heart Set Free*, pp. 363, 364.

[3] White, *The Acts of the Apostles*, p. 431.

[4] *Ibid.*, pp. 434, 435.

The Dawn of Hope for the World

Acts 26:1-32

In the English spring the morning rings with bird-calls. Before the early riser can pick out any brightening of the eastern horizon, the birds have sensed the approaching dawn.

Clocks and watches cannot tell the moment of first dawn. Not even the observatory can be precise. But the birds know and announce it to the world.

In one of the most beautiful pictures in the New Testament, Jesus rises from death to announce the dawn of salvation to Hebrew and Gentile alike (Acts 26:23).

The Hope and the Promise
Acts 26:1-8

The story of Agrippa arouses some sympathy for this member of the Herod family. Like the rich young ruler, circumstances have him in their power. Not that Agrippa displayed the high moral character that a Jewish leader should. History records how the people gossiped about his relationship with his sister Bernice. In fact, not long after Paul's defense she married and moved away from her brother. But less than four years later she returned to him.

Luke presents Paul's defense before Agrippa as the most important of the five recorded in the last chapters of Acts. We might call this passage "Paul's Purpose for His Life."

The description of the pomp and splendor of the

court heightens the importance of the occasion. Agrippa and Festus provided the very setting in which Paul might present the essentials of God's commission to rulers and princes (Acts 25:23).

Luke's account picks up three important themes: (1) the process that had begun two years before established Paul's innocence (Acts 25:25; 26:31); (2) the Jewish king, who outranked the high priest and the Sanhedrin, also accepted Paul's innocence (verse 32); and (3) a large group of officials, both Jewish and Gentile, heard the verdict of innocent (Acts 25:23).

Paul presented the gospel positively and with an appeal to accept Jesus Christ. Like Peter's speech at Pentecost and Stephen's to the Sanhedrin, his sermon provided a model for other Christian evangelists to follow.

The apostle's *kerygma* ("proclamation") plead for repentance (Acts 26:20), declared forgiveness (verse 18), and called for righteous deeds (verse 20). Jesus Christ provided light to both Jew and Gentile (verse 23), as foretold by the prophets and Moses (verse 22). The public nature of Christ's ministry and resurrection (verse 26) opened the appeal of the gospel to all (verse 29). The facts about Jesus demanded response and trust in Him (verse 27).

Like the English today, the Romans had a good sense of ceremony. Agrippa gave formal permission to begin, and Paul responded just as formally (verse 1). How different this beginning to the sharp interchange in the presence of the high priest (Acts 23:1-3) and to the mob at the steps of the fortress of Antonia (Acts 21:35, 36).

Paul had a judge who knew enough about the Jewish religion to evaluate what he would say (Acts 26:2, 3). Festus had already determined Paul innocent of any capital crime (Acts 25:25).

Paul first established his Jewish credentials (Acts 26:4, 5). Elsewhere he had described himself as "exceedingly zealous" in his religion, more so than many of his fellow religionists (Gal. 1:14).

The Pharisee link obviously had importance (Acts 26:5). He described his interpretation of the Law as being that of a Pharisee (cf. Phil. 3:5). The possibility of winning many Pharisees to Christian belief is a feature of Acts. They found the teaching about the resurrection reassuring and also appreciated the emphasis on fulfillment of prophecy.

Paul linked inseparably the hope of the Messiah with that of the resurrection (Acts 26:7, 8). The Messiah must be the Lifegiver, even though suffering death Himself. Resurrection linked vicarious atonement with eternal life.

Yet the ones who hope for the promise of Messiah impeached the one who proclaimed the truth about Him. By putting the words *by Jews* at the end of his argument (verse 7), Paul pointed to the peculiar turn of events that now put his freedom and even his life at risk.

The prophets taught Israel to hope. Again and again in the nation's history despair had turned to elation. Deliverers arose; miracles transformed circumstances. Interpreting this, the prophets saw the saving acts of God as a continuing part of the covenant. Israel must do her part; but the people seldom questioned God's willingness to redeem the nation. In Jesus, Paul said, the hope of Israel found its ultimate fulfillment. The 12 tribes (verse 7) practiced their religion in order to assure the fulfillment of hope. Paul saw that hope answered beyond expectation in Jesus. His resurrection provided the final proof that Israel served the God of hope. Salvation had come in Jesus the Messiah (cf. Rom. 5:1, 2).

> "My hope is built on nothing less
> Than Jesus' blood and righteousness;
> I dare not trust the sweetest frame,
> But wholly lean on Jesus' name.
> On Christ, the solid Rock, I stand;

All other ground is sinking sand,
All other ground is sinking sand." [1]

The Pharisee might answer Paul's question (Acts 26:8) with "we do believe He can raise the dead." But that missed the point. Paul asked why they accepted the belief in principle, but denied it in the most important case—the resurrection of Jesus. Why, he was asking, should Israel turn from its longed-for hope?

The New Testament gives no grounds for believing the fable of the 10 *lost* tribes. Paul's reference to the 12 (verse 7) shows that the Jews themselves did not accept such an interpretation. The New Testament sees Israel as one nation, not as two *known* tribes and a *lost* 10 (Matt. 19:28; Luke 22:30; James 1:1; Rev. 7:4-6; 21:12).

Belief and Action
Acts 26:9-18

Once Paul had refused to consider the question If God could not raise Jesus, why believe in the resurrection at all? In fact, he had accepted the responsibility of eliminating from Judaism the teaching about Jesus (Acts 26:9).

Paul visited local synagogues (verse 10), forcing a vote on the fate of Christians. Each synagogue had the right to make determinations regarding matters of the Law of Moses. He did not necessarily succeed in making them blaspheme (verse 11). The Greek speaks of an attempt to do this rather than success in forcing them. The future apostle sought to create doubt and force despair (verse 11). But even in the face of his cruelty believers in Jesus remained faithful.

Stephen's arguments may have been more convincing than Saul the persecutor was prepared to admit. The faith of the Christians worried him. As a Jew from the Dispersion he may have been impressed by Stephen's argument against the limitations of Temple worship. The forceful presentation of God's freedom to bless and establish His presence wherever He chose meant much to him.

Now Paul added new material in this third telling of the Damascus road encounter: (1) the light was brighter than the sun (verse 13); (2) it flashed around him and his companions (verse 13); (3) all fell to the ground (verse 14); and (4) the voice from above used Hebrew. Such details created a picture of the force of the event and helped explain why it had so radically affected him.

Contemporary Jewish belief held that God sent voices from heaven to reprove and correct. But the Gentiles needed an explanation of how a Jew would react to such an event (verses 14, 15). Paul addressed Jesus as "Lord" (verse 15). Through a common vision experience he came to the same conclusion as Stephen—the resurrected Jesus reigns with God.

God's purpose for Paul (verse 16) had two parts: servant and witness. 1. As witness Paul was to emphasize what Jesus had shown and told him. His personal experience with Jesus would be the key to his success. And Jesus promised further revelations. 2. As servant he would fulfill a prophetic role as defined in the servant passage in Isaiah 42:6, 7, 16. The servant model of ministry dominates the New Testament. Those who minister pattern their service on Jesus, the suffering servant (Isa. 53).

Jesus had been delivered up to crucifixion and death (Matt. 27:26). Paul would suffer, but also escape many times from both the Jewish people and the Gentiles (Acts 26:17). By delivering His servants God fulfills His mission for them.

Those who have faith in Him Jesus will rescue from the power of Satan (verse 18; cf. Col. 1:13, 14). Jesus was still talking to Paul. The words gave identity to a new Israel, set apart or "sanctified by faith that is in me" (verse

18). All who trusted in Jesus will receive "inheritance among them" who make up the true people of God.

Mission and Its Meaning
Acts 26:19-32

In contrast with Agrippa, the figure of Paul rises to titanic proportions. Paul obeyed the heavenly vision (Acts 26:19). "The chances are that Agrippa never had any great visions, and the ones he may have had were soon lost among the innumerable and competing interests of his life. Paul had a vision which he did nothing to create or deserve, but once he had it, he was obedient to it to the very end. It was in the obedience that the grandeur of Paul was to be found. . . . Not perfection could he claim before Agrippa, but obedience." [2]

The obedience that he showed (verses 19, 20) is asked by the Lord of all whom He sanctifies and forgives. Repentance by words alone means little; deeds of repentance count.

When Paul attempted to give meaning to his mission, trouble broke out (verse 21). The call to repent and find faith in Jesus Christ angered many Jerusalem Jews. They hated him for daring to suggest that when God had sent the Messiah they had not discerned or accepted Him, but killed Him. Perhaps if the apostle had confined the call to Jews, they would have tolerated him. God had sent many prophets to call the nation to repent. But Paul went further. He offered salvation on an equal basis to Jew and Gentile (verse 23).

The reasons Paul gave for the attack in the Temple (verse 21) are: (1) his change from enemy of the Christians to their most eloquent evangelist (verse 19); (2) his proclamation of Jesus as Lord (verse 15); (3) his mission to the Gentiles (verse 17); (4) his declaration of an inheritance for the Gentiles (verse 18); and (5) his teaching that Gentiles might repent and have their good deeds acknowledged (verse 20). The Christian witness reinterpreted Jewish expectations (verses 22, 23). "Despite occasional claims to the contrary, there is no evidence that pre-Christian Judaism ever thought of the Messiah in terms of suffering. Certainly many of the building blocks for a later doctrine of a suffering Messiah were present.... But the proclamation of both a suffering Messiah and the resurrection of Jesus were distinctive to early Christianity. . . . Such features of the Christian message went beyond the beliefs and expectations of Judaism." [3]

Paul's sermon now reached its climax. Jesus fulfilled all that the prophets spoke (verse 22; cf. Luke 24:27, 44). Agrippa, a Jew, would understand the force of the arguments. If we had the full text of the speech, we would know precisely which scripture Paul used, but we have seen many examples in Acts already. The critical teachings declared that the Messiah must suffer, die, and rise again.

And so through Paul God was announcing the dawn to a world captive to darkness in the domain of Satan (Acts 26:18, 23). The Sun of Righteousness was shedding His rays into the court of Agrippa. Would anyone see the light?

How could Festus really understand an address presented in a Jewish framework? Shouting, he stopped Paul dead (verse 24). The Roman governor knew how the rabbis studied and studied. Obviously study had pushed Paul too far and he had gone over into fantasy. Men or women who feel threatened by the gospel react much the same. It appears to ask too much of them. Vicarious death and the resurrection seem a strange dream painted by a surrealist painter.

Not so, Paul replied, these are true and reasonable words (verse 25). Agrippa knows I am speaking the truth. The facts are not hidden (verse 26). The apostle could have directed his presentation to the Gentile mind of Festus, but he felt that Agrippa would respond best.

"These words [verse 26] light up Luke's presentation

in Acts from beginning to end: the risen Lord was 40 days with his disciples and went to heaven before many witnesses. At Pentecost thousands (Acts 2:41) experienced the mighty coming of the Spirit and its effect. The apostles worked miracles before all the people (Acts 3:9; 5:15; 19:11f.) and spoke to thousands of listeners (Acts 4:4). . . . The entire history of Christianity—it is no secret society!—is enacted publicly and before high and exalted personages. Christianity is not an inconspicuous event any longer, but a factor in world history." [4]

To Agrippa's "You almost bring me to the point of playing the Christian," Paul had an answer. He saw the king vacillating between yes and no, between seriousness and humor, and replied, "May you all be like I am, sooner or later"—and that would include Agrippa, Bernice, Festus, and the entire assembly—"except for these chains" (verse 29).

The impressive presentation finished, the king, the governor, and their counselors talked it over (verses 30, 31). The conclusion assessed not just Paul but all Christianity. Paul should live, and that without punishment (verse 31). Christianity should have freedom, without restrictions.

But there remained the matter of the appeal to Caesar, and that must proceed (verse 32). Again, not just Paul but Christianity itself must go to Caesar. Divine programming has taken over, and all the public events of Acts will now climax with the great Paul before Caesar in Rome. There, too, judgments might be made in favor not just of Paul but of Christianity.

We know that for Paul it did not work out as the flow of Acts might lead us to expect. The apostle would suffer at the order of the very person who should have heard him. But even though he died at the caprice of the emperor, his work was not stopped or limited. His influence spreads and prospers among us today. Nor did the cruelty of pagan Rome black out the dawn of hope. The plan of God and the directing of the Spirit brought forth the world-saving message of the gospel, which shines upon all people and gives the bright hope of eternal life.

---

[1] Edward Mote, "My Hope Is Built on Nothing Less," *The SDA Hymnal,* No. 522.

[2] *The Interpreter's Bible,* vol. 9, p. 328.

[3] Gaebelein, ed., *The Expositor's Bible Commentary,* vol. 9, p. 554.

[4] Haenchen, *The Acts of the Apostles,* pp. 691, 692.

Do Not
Lose Heart

Acts 27:1-28:31

In the conquest of space man has made progressive sorties from our envelope of life-supporting gas into the void beyond. Earth may provide a base for colonies of humans on the moon or even on Mars.

Looking back to those nights in 1957 when keen eyes isolated the moving spot of light called Sputnik, that time seems both near and distant. The memory is vivid enough, but we remember, too, the years between. With unbelievable technology we shared the wonder of launching objects into orbit. Intrepid spacemen showed us what it is like to walk and drive on the moon. And yes, we recall the tragedies and near tragedies that remind us that new frontiers are always established at great cost.

Acts and the growth of early Christianity moved the apostles step-by-step from the support system of Jerusalem and Judaism. Looking back, we now realize that Luke had a specific destination in mind. The shorter sorties had the longer in view. He wanted to put Paul in Rome as the proclaimer of a widely accepted and all-embracing faith.

The tone of Acts 27 and 28 moves away from successful evangelism and careful defense of the faith to the providences of God. And the arrival in Rome produced none of the citywide uproar that we have learned to expect. The reaction to his arrival, positive as it may have been, was muted.

What, then, is Luke stressing? First, chapter 27, with its

miracle-strewn voyage to Rome, demonstrates that when God has a purpose, whatever happens, through human or other causes, will not divert that plan. We may think of the voyage as a physical parallel to the spiritual journey already recorded in the previous chapters. Second, Paul in Rome is climax enough without the expected audience with Caesar. Jesus pressed on to Jerusalem regardless (Luke 9:50, 51), because in Jerusalem what the prophets had foretold would come true. In Acts the story moves just as inexorably toward Rome because there the promise of Jesus about the uttermost ends of the earth and the prophecies about light to the Gentiles would find their authentication.

Disaster and Deliverance
Acts 27:1-44

The journey to Rome (Acts 27:1-5) charts the course of the Christian church: tossed this way and that, with threats ahead (verse 10), but still the only way to fulfill the divine purpose. The storms and threatened mutiny parallel Jesus' conflicts with the scribes. The shipwreck stands in place of the Passion, and the deliverance and final arrival in Rome parallels the Resurrection. The geography of faith has ever been thus. The church and its people gain the kingdom with difficulty and only through divine providence.

But this does not turn the shipwreck story into allegory, which it is not, nor is it parable. The multifaceted skills of Luke used historical incidents to make a point about God's purposes and His providences that all should heed.

The detail of the journey has provided source material for scholars studying trade routes and weather patterns in the Mediterranean. Luke is accurate and detailed. As one of the "we" passages in Acts, it carries the conviction and incident of a personal experience.

Paul's first advice met no response (verse 10). Since it

was the third shipwreck for Paul (2 Cor. 11:25), he was in a position to give suggestions on how to deal with it. The centurion, Julius, like all other centurions in Luke's volumes, was a good, fair, and kindly man (Acts 27:3). However, he heeded the ship captain rather than Paul (verse 11).

The ship nearly foundered. No sail could hold it into the wind (verse 15). Driven by the same wind, the ship's boat made wild dashes of its own, straining the cables, plowing in and out of the waves, and driving at the ship itself (verse 16). Good seamanship not only hoisted it on board but also passed hawsers under and around the ship to prevent the planks from parting (verse 17). The vessel drove on (verse 18), like a giant waterborne parcel, tied around with rope and at the mercy of the winds.

God was not without alternate plans (verses 21-26). Once He had established the ultimate goal (verse 24), neither tempest nor human error could alter it. A handful of right-living people might have preserved Sodom and Gomorrah. For this ship's crew, it took one Paul to save the lot.

"The apostle, though himself suffering physically, had words of hope for the darkest hour, a helping hand in every emergency. . . . He had no fears for himself; he knew that God would preserve him to witness at Rome for the truth of Christ. But his heart yearned with pity for the poor souls around him, sinful, degraded, and unprepared to die." [1]

The Bible does not give the occasion when Paul was "brought before Caesar" (verse 24). That his witness there brought success we know from Philippians 1:13, 14; 4:22. The apostle understood the political importance of Rome as he reached toward Spain and the western ends of the empire.

Paul knew that he was as near to God on the sea as he was on land.

"O Christ, whose voice the waters heard,
And hushed their raging at Thy word,
Who walkedst on the foaming deep,
And calm amidst its rage didst sleep;
Oh, hear us when we cry to Thee
For those in peril on the sea." [2]

Luke portrays his brief speeches aboard the storm-tossed craft as having great significance:

1. His first speech underlined his status as a prophet of God (Acts 27:10). God's people have a prophetic message to this rudderless world.

2. The life-saving promise (verses 21-26) had another level besides the physical one. He would also appear in the debauched and adrift household of Caesar and give spiritual life. The word of witness still stands against the drift to immorality.

3. His command to all on board to eat used words similar to the Lord's Supper (verses 31-35). Luke's description recalls a pastor at the Communion service (verse 35). Who, with Christ at his side, may not remain calm in the face of the gravest danger? And are not such the very ones to call the world to "eat" the Word before destruction comes?

Throughout the storm the captain took step after step to avert disaster:

1. He let the ship run before the Euroclydon—the tempest that blasted out of the northeast (verse 15).

2. He had the ship's boat hauled on board and hawsers placed around the girth of the vessel (verse 17).

3. He ordered the sails struck so that they might escape being driven onto the quicksands and shoals of Syrtis (verse 17).

4. He took careful soundings to indicate the approach of land (verse 28).

5. He had stern anchors dropped to provide a sure hold against the gale (verse 29).

6. He had wheat shoveled overboard to lighten the ship (verse 38).

7. He directed the crew to make an attempt at running the vessel up a creek mouth (verse 39).

Without Christ all efforts to save oneself or another are futile. But with faith in Him all efforts to destroy and deny hope are equally futile.

A study of the coasts of Malta gives only one possible place where a creek lies in view and large bodies of the sea meet (verse 41). A narrow channel runs between Malta and the island of Salmone, which shelters Saint Paul's Bay. The sticky clay on the sea bottom would hold the ship's prow toward the shore while waves battered the stern to pieces.

Modern critics state that vipers do not live on Malta and that the island has little wood. However, the past might have been quite different from today. Ireland has no snakes, though once they seem to have been plentiful. The presence of continuous agriculture can radically alter the limited ecology of an island.

Luke's quiet humor comes through in this passage as he depicts the superstitions of the islanders and the sudden switch in their view of Paul. In minutes he went from a man pursued by divine justice (Acts 28:2, 3) to a being of divine origin (verse 6). But unlike the Lystrans (Acts 14:13), the islanders made no attempt to worship Paul (Acts 28:6), and the incident passed without further action by him.

And So to Rome
Acts 28:1-31

Because Luke did not always accompany Paul on his journeys, we do not always sense the physician in him as he writes. But Malta is different. Paul's healing gifts soon had the populace flocking to him. A hint appears that Luke may have assisted professionally. The islanders honored "us," not just Paul (Acts 28:10).

"The malady the father of Publius was suffering from may have been Malta fever. . . . Cases of Malta fever are long-lasting—an average of four months, but in some cases lasting two or three years. Paul uses the plural *pyretois* in his description, probably with reference to the way it affects its victims with intermittent attacks." [3]

While we may regard the Malta experience as minor, it revived the aging Paul and prepared him for Rome and the fulfillment of God's plan for him. The discovery of Christians at Puteoli and the two delegations that met him at Appii Forum and Three Taverns gave him courage (verses 14, 15).

"Appii Forum is 43 miles (69 kilometers) from Rome and the Three Taverns, 33 (53 kilometers). They were on the great Appian Way, which led from Rome to the coast. And a deputation of Roman Christians came to meet him. The Greek word used is that used for a conqueror. They came to meet Paul as one of the great ones of the earth." [4]

In describing his own fate (verses 17-20) Paul's language came close to that used of Jesus' (Luke 18:32). Luke may have wanted us to see once more the parallels between Paul's experience and that of the Saviour. The apostle stated that he had "committed nothing against the people, or customs of our fathers" (Acts 28:17).

The Romans would have liked to release him (verse 18). Festus may have thought that two years in detention satisfied any misdemeanor Paul might have committed. But the Jews objected to his release (verse 19), forcing Paul to appeal to Caesar rather than face a trial at Jerusalem (Acts 25:11).

The resurrection of Jesus has changed forever the defining of hope (Acts 28:20). Because Jesus rose, so will the faithful (1 Cor. 15:20, 21). Paul foresaw the final gathering of the Israel of God so that all Israel will be saved (Rom. 11:26). What the salvation of all Israel will mean, the prophet foretells (Rev. 7:9). The mighty tree of salvation grows and grows as the Lord adds branches from every nation, kindred, tongue, and people (Rom. 11:24).

The Jews of Jerusalem had not pursued their victim to Rome (verse 21). The failure of his tormentors to follow him may have been because they felt no need now that the Romans had Paul in their hands or because the Romans dealt severely with claimants who had ill-prepared or weak cases.

Paul had freedom to preach and teach (verses 30, 31). At his invitation large numbers came to his house. Both Jesus and Paul, in their final episodes, taught from the Law and the Prophets (verse 23; Luke 24:44). Such teaching did not always convince, even when testified to by direct witnesses such as Cleopas and Paul (Luke 24:18, 25-27, 36-38; Acts 26:16), but some accepted the testimony (Acts 28:24).

Many have wished that Luke had told us more. What did happen to Paul? We know he died a martyr's death in Nero's pogrom against Christians in A.D. 66. The two years of verse 30 would bring us to A.D. 61. Ellen G. White gives us a picture of a trial soon over and Paul released. He then journeyed again among the churches of Greece. On his return to Rome he was arrested, tried, and executed. During this period he wrote the pastoral Epistles.

Luke has reached his climax. He closes with the story open-ended. Preaching and persuading, Paul moves into an unspecified future. So does the church. Because the Spirit lives as the One between the witness and the world, the world not only must, but will, in part, hear and obey. Paul is the servant of that Spirit, as are we. We face a future about which we can fix no dates nor measure the expectations of God for the gospel He has given through His Son, our Lord and Saviour, Jesus Christ.

[1] White, *The Acts of the Apostles*, p. 442.

[2] William Whiting, "Eternal Father, Strong to Save," *The SDA Hymnal*, No. 85.

[3] Gaebelein, ed., *The Expositor's Bible Commentary*, vol. 9, p. 565.

[4] William Barclay, *The Acts of the Apostles: The Daily Study Bible*, p. 190.

Luke the Lord's Man

Luke has trumpeted the success of God's great heroes. Peter and Paul lead the parade of the great witnesses of the gospel. He has shown their great deeds, recorded the impact of their lives.

But not them alone. The New Testament writer has also saluted men and women whose less eventful lives have nonetheless had staggering effects on the advance of Christianity. Through him we have heard how Stephen levered the church out from its Jerusalem base toward its world mission with dire results to himself. Philip has shown us what it means to be blown by the Holy Wind. Cornelius has accepted the unique role given him.

We have met Dorcas and Ananias, who in their own ways also set in motion unfinished blessings. Apollo has flamed briefly through the pages of Acts lighting the world he evangelized. Priscilla and Aquila have partnered Paul at critical moments of service. Barnabas has gentled the troubled and consoled the uncertain.

But we would have it wrong if we for a moment accuse Luke of hero worship or simply writing the stuff of saint stories. He has a different purpose. The Lord's man, he presents Jesus Christ as his only true hero. One does not have to read long in Luke to discover that the physician had his personal interest in Jesus.

We know practically nothing about the author's life. What evidence there is suggests that he was a Gentile physician, perhaps trained in Philippi but based in

Antioch. His interests and emphasis suggest his Gentile background. His technical language supports his medical knowledge. And the way he makes Antioch the locus from which the missionary journeys radiate indicates a special interest in the city.

If he was a Gentile—and that seems almost certain—he is the only non-Jewish writer in the whole Bible. After Paul, he has written more of the New Testament than anyone else. In his books he expresses his strong conviction that God has events—personal, contemporary, and future—under control.

In Christ, Luke saw how God worked out His purposes (Luke 22:42). He deplored the Jewish leaders who refused God's purpose for them (Luke 7:30). Accompanying Paul on some of the most dangerous of his adventures, he stood nearby in Jerusalem when the crowd nearly pulled the apostle apart. He boarded the ill-fated voyage to Rome. Life with Paul taught him the power God had vested in Jesus Christ, and he wrote it in his Gospel and his church history.

Jesus Who Reigns on High

"The Lord said to my Lord, 'Sit at my right hand until I make your enemies your footstool,' " Luke has Peter quoting (Acts 2:34, 35, NEB). Holding a high view of Jesus Christ, Luke rejected contemporary suggestions that reduced Jesus to a remarkable man whom God in some way had elevated to divine status. He also denied the opposite point of view that Jesus was a divine being who masked his origins and appeared as a man.

Because He is at the right hand of God, He rules with and as God (Acts 7:44). Though he does not spell it out, as Paul later did, Luke would not feel uncomfortable to hear Jesus addressed as God. In Acts Paul addresses Jesus as "Lord" (Acts 26:15).

Luke insists on the historical evidence that showed the human nature of Jesus. He proclaims the historical

Jesus who died, but whose flesh never suffered corruption (Acts 2:31). This Jesus of human flesh was raised and exalted to the right hand of God (verse 33).

Therefore Luke found special interest in studying how Jesus dealt with the pressures of His human existence. He recorded more occasions when Jesus prayed than any other gospel writer. Only he brings us to Gethsemane to observe the drops of blood falling from Jesus' brow. Expecting and finding that the early disciples prayed frequently, he shared in those prayers (Acts 21:5). The beloved physician also had a clear view of where his prayers went. Christ at the Father's side meant that he had access to Jesus, just as His followers had while He was on earth.

Jesus the Helper

At the very moment when the noblest of defenders of the faith sank under a hail of stones, Jesus reached out to help him. "I can see the Son of Man standing at God's right hand!" (Acts 7:56, NEB). In his gospel, Luke had faithfully recorded Jesus' promise about acknowledging those who trusted Him before the Father. In Acts he records an actual example.

The incident demonstrated that God accepted him because of Jesus' ministry and that Jesus, the eternal Son at the right hand of God, could receive him and assure him eternal life.

Conversion means "trusting in Jesus" or "having faith in Jesus." Faith in Jesus' name performs the key miracles of Acts. Luke therefore saw Jesus as the ever-present and involved One, ready to move on behalf of all who would, even in the weakest way, put their trust in Him.

In Acts important people found faith in Jesus and listened respectfully to those who spoke of Him. However, Luke never forgot what the life of Jesus had taught him: both immeasurable need and overwhelming response may be found in the simple, poor, and deprived people of the world (Luke 15:1, 2). He was not just defending Christianity as he described this response and noted the reasons for it, but was also reflecting his own personal conviction that human barriers of race, language, sex, and wealth had no place in any worthwhile system of human values.

God is an interventionist. He steps in, intrudes, changes. We can trust Him to watch events, to make sure that none of His plans go awry. Luke was no deist, holding that God kept aloof and had no interest in human affairs. Rather, God is a personal being and Jesus remains a human person. The compassion and concern He showed on earth is an essential part of His nature even now.

Without doubt Luke loved people. Of all the gospel writers he best captures Jesus the helper who loved all and sought to bring them life. In Acts his writing urges the church onward with its task. People are waiting for salvation, and the witnesses must hurry with the message of love. The selfish and the religious quacks who fatten on the poor and credulous receive short shrift. Ananias and Sapphira, Simon Magus, Elymas, and the sons of Sceva—like the Pharisees of the Gospel—used things and people for selfish purposes. But Luke had no more time for them than Jesus had for the hypocrite and the deceitful.

The Skills of Luke

Luke, the Lord's man, devoted his skills to exalting Jesus. He completed his Gospel and the Acts around A.D. 61 or 62. Historical events that we can check externally we find slotted in correctly. In this he makes a vital point about his Lord: Jesus lived and ministered in Judea about 30 years before. He was a real person. You can know what He was like from my history. The church in touch with Jesus learns its lessons from Him, carries on His mission.

However, Luke gathers theological significance as he departs from other Gospel authors and adds new material, or rearranges shared material. His chief purposes are those of the historian and storyteller. But do not limit him. He has and expresses theological concerns. A cohesive thought system about Christianity lies behind his writing, into which he fits history and story. The latter conveys his theology in a natural flow of thought that speaks of careful analysis and confident grasp of information.

For Luke Jesus came to seek and to save the lost. For him the mission of the church is that also. Everything flows out from that key concept, which exalts Jesus and His saving power in a way that has encouraged and strengthened Christianity for nearly 2,000 years.

Jesus and the Spirit

Luke knew the Spirit. He had noted how the Spirit operated between Jesus and the world; he knew that the same Spirit was between him and the task that he was doing for God. Luke was the Spirit's man.

The New Testament writer could not conceive of any divine action among humanity that excluded the Spirit. From the first verses of the Gospel to the end of Acts, the Spirit is going between God and the needy world to ensure His purposes.

In the first chapters of Luke, the Spirit activates all. Because of Him the holy Child enters the world, and all things change. Once Luke has declared Jesus full of the Spirit, he leaves it there. He will not have us believe that Jesus and the Spirit can ever have different goals. They are one. Paul captured Luke's thought when he wrote "the Lord is that Spirit" (2 Cor. 3:17).

Because Jesus and the Spirit are one—because the Spirit comes from God—Luke may speak of Jesus' sending the Spirit (Acts 2:32, 33). The oneness of Jesus and the Spirit, which made the Lord's life so powerful and effective, has never been driven asunder. Jesus and the Spirit remain one in heaven as they were on earth.

Therefore, to trust in Jesus means to receive the Spirit.

Luke brings Jesus back to earth in the presence of the Spirit. True, He reigns at the right hand of the Father, but through the Spirit He works within the church and the world with all the power of His earthly ministry. Those who do their work in the name of Jesus are participating through the Spirit in the power of Jesus. The Spirit does nothing of Himself, but gives Jesus to the witnesses and to the world.

Luke himself had received the Spirit, and thus had been put in touch with Jesus. As a member of the band of witnesses, he found his most effective witness in providing authentic reports of what had happened and was even now continuing. And he did it under the discipline and guidance of the Spirit sent from Jesus.

The devout people with whom the Spirit delights to dwell help us understand the character of Luke. Their piety and humility attracted him, and on them he must have modeled his own life.

As the Lord's man Luke emerges from the mists of history. We have no idea of his physical appearance, but we do know that he reflected the image of his Maker. No one could have written so carefully and so passionately of all that Jesus had done without being deeply involved.

Clearly he loved his Lord and delighted in the work of the Spirit. In Acts he has given us much of permanent value. Of the many things we might mention, here are a few.

1. The most important task of the church is its mission. Luke focuses on mission and witness. One might therefore conclude that a church that pauses too long to reflect on its inner life may lose rather than gain.

2. Anyone who wants to understand the history of the church should consider the people who created that history and how it affected them. The church is about people; Luke saw that clearly.

3. Luke declares that racial and other forms of

discrimination have no part in the Christian outreach, a fact that he reminds us of over and over.

4. Mission does not achieve through human endeavor but through the presence of the Spirit. He is in us and between us and the world so that His mission might succeed.

5. Luke believes in the triumph of the gospel and of the church that proclaims it. God pushes aside hindrances and rides over obstacles as the church moves toward the appointed goal.

6. God is creating His own redemptive history that both stands aside from and incorporates secular history. The church fulfills and accomplishes that redemptive history. Prophecy has been fulfilled in Jesus Christ. Now the church both fulfills prophecy and speaks of the future coming of Jesus.

7. The speeches of Acts, the way the church dealt with problems, the methods used by the witnesses—all teach us. We learn from their example.

Luke loved his Lord and loved the church his Lord had commissioned. He wanted it to go into the future both informed and united. The church is the Lord's creation and will prosper only as it serves and obeys Him.

And Luke looked forward. The Lord had not yet come, and work still lay at hand. Just as he authored the Gospel with the future of the followers of Jesus in view, so he wrote Acts. The raising of Jesus to the presence of the Father thrilled him. He anticipated the day when Jesus would return and gather those who trusted in Him to the Father's presence.

To Luke's purposes and hopes the Spirit has said yes. Luke saw the Spirit as the God who works in between the church and the world to fulfill the purposes of God. He will, perhaps, not be too surprised to discover that the same Spirit has used him and his writing. He was, after all, the Lord's man, as we also must be, willing to let the Spirit of the Lord work within us as He chooses.